MIND AND BRAIN

MIND AND BRAIN

A Dialogue on the Mind-Body Problem

Rocco J. Gennaro

Hackett Publishing Company, Inc.
Indianapolis/Cambridge

00 99 98   2 3 4 5

For further information, please address

Hackett Publishing Company, Inc.
P.O. Box 44937
Indianapolis, Indiana 46244-0937

Cover design by John Pershing and Shawn Woodyard

Text design by Dan Kirklin

Library of Congress Cataloging-in-Publication Data

Gennaro, Rocco J.
    Mind and brain: a dialogue on the mind-body problem/ Rocco J.
Gennaro.
        p.   cm.
    Includes bibliographical references.
    ISBN 0–87220–332–8 (pbk)   ISBN 0–87220–333–6 (cloth)
    1. Dualism.   2. Mind and body   3. Philosophy of mind
I. Title.
B812.G46   1996
128'.2—dc20   95–46249
                                           CIP

The paper used in this publication meets the minimum requirements of
American National Standard for Information Sciences—Permanence of Paper for Printed Library Materials, ANSI Z39.48-1984.

∞

CONTENTS

INTRODUCTION

This dialogue is an introduction to the mind-body problem and is intended for use in philosophy and psychology courses. Its purpose is to develop some of the views and arguments that have emerged in the literature. For those not familiar with the philosophy of mind, the dialogue aims to provide an overview of the key issues; it can also serve as a summary for those with a broader background. No prior knowledge of philosophy is required.

There are three characters and "three nights" of debate or conversation. The reader can easily remember which position each participant holds by the first letter of his or her name, e.g. *M*ary is the *m*aterialist and *D*ave is the *d*ualist. The First Night covers (1) introductory terminology; (2) the connection of the mind-body problem to immortality; (3) the scientific advantages of materialism; (4) a critical discussion of Descartes' "Divisibility Argument" for dualism; and (5) a critical discussion of what is called the "Argument from Introspection."

The Second Night covers (1) problems with dualism concerning the interaction between the mind and the brain; (2) a critical discussion of parallelism; (3) the so-called type/token distinction within materialism; and (4) a discussion of well-known arguments from Thomas Nagel and Frank Jackson against materialism with respect to its ability to explain consciousness.

The Third Night focuses on the more epistemological "Problem of Other Minds." I examine (1) the difference between inductive and certain knowledge; (2) how the problem changes depending on whether the "other mind" is human, animal, alien or machine; (3) various kinds of evidence which might help to determine whether another creature has a mind, e.g. behavior and brain structure; and (4) a version of the so-called Inverted Spectrum Argument.

Key terms or principles and the names of arguments are printed in **bold**; other emphasized words are in *italics*. There are also numerous study questions and a selected bibliography with notes.

I would like to thank Michael Patton, C.L. Hardin, Paul Sauer, Mark O. Webb and Neil Manson for helpful comments on an earlier draft of this manuscript.

Rocco J. Gennaro
Indiana State University

MIND AND BRAIN

A Dialogue on the Mind-Body Problem

This is a record of conversations among three first-year philosophy graduate students about the nature of the mind. The conversations take place in a graduate student pub over three nights. Mary, a materialist, is arguing with Dave, a dualist, about the relevance of their beliefs to the issue of immortality. Steve, who is generally skeptical of both positions and less certain of his own view, joins Mary and Dave later.

THE FIRST NIGHT

DAVE: What's wrong, Mary?

MARY: Well, I found out just last night that my cousin Tom has died after a short battle with cancer. It's been difficult for everyone in the family to accept.

DAVE: I'm very sorry. I know how you feel. My sister died of leukemia last year. We all miss her terribly, but she is always with me, and I know that I'll see her again someday. Perhaps you can take some comfort in the idea that Tom is in Heaven. I believe in God and immortality. Do you?

MARY: No. There are many reasons why I do not believe in God. For example, I have a difficult time understanding why a supposedly all-knowing, all-powerful, and all-good Being would allow so much misery and evil to exist in the world. I know that theists have a reply to this "problem of evil," but they have not convinced me. However, this is not the main reason for my atheism.

DAVE: What is your main reason, then?

MARY: Since I don't believe in immortality, I find it difficult to believe in God, especially as represented in the western conception of God. I mean, if our death really is the end, then why believe in God? What would be the point? I think that a belief in immortality is prior to a belief in God. *Psychologically* speaking, I think that it is the desire for continued life after bodily death that ultimately leads most people to believe in God. I know, of course, that there are independent *philosophical* arguments put forth to show that God exists, but that is a different issue. I also think they fail to establish the existence of God. But what I am saying here is that, as a matter of psychological fact, a belief in immortality is often the main motivation for a belief in God.

DAVE: I think there are good independent reasons to believe in God, but I'm curious about your reasoning here. Since your atheism derives mainly from your not believing in immortality, I must ask why you are so sure there is no life after death.

MARY: Because I am a **materialist** about the human mind, i.e. I believe that all mental processes are simply brain processes or states. In short, the mind is the brain.

DAVE: How do you then conclude that there is no immortality?

MARY: Well, what is it that continues on after bodily death? Clearly, it is supposed to be one's thoughts, memories, beliefs, experiences, etc. And isn't this what we mean by the 'mind'? But if the mind is the brain, then at death it must cease to exist and must eventually rot away with the rest of the body. Therefore, there cannot be immortality.

DAVE: I follow your reasoning, but aren't you confusing the mind with the soul? I believe it is the soul that survives bodily death.

MARY: When we describe what is supposed to be immortal, it sounds like what we mean by the mind. I defy you to explain any coherent distinction between the mind and the soul. As a matter of fact, these terms are used interchangeably in many historical texts, and, for example, both English words are used to translate the single Greek word '*psyche*'. Granted, sometimes the term 'soul' carries a more theological connotation, but it doesn't follow that the words 'soul' and 'mind' refer to entirely different things.

DAVE: I'll accept your equation of 'mind' with 'soul' for the sake of argument, but I am not sure there is no difference. For example, I believe that infants, fetuses, and severely mentally defective people have souls that are just as real and whole as yours or mine. But clearly their minds are not. Moreover, in the case of most unborn children there is no mind at all yet in the sense that you have described. Also, many animals have minds but do not have souls.

MARY: So there are three things associated with each human being: a mind, a soul, and a body?

DAVE: Yes. On second thought, you may be right that there are only two. I'll have to think about it some more.

MARY: It sounds awfully crowded in your view of human beings. I have a hard time accepting such a position, especially if you want to hold that the mind or the soul or both are nonphysical in some way. Is this what you think?

DAVE: Yes. I am a **substance dualist:** I believe that the mind and the body are distinct substances, and that the mind is a nonphysical substance.

MARY: Do you again see how the mind sounds like the soul?

DAVE: Sure. I said I'd grant you that, for the sake of argument. But you see, of course, why I believe in immortality. If my mind is nonphysical, then it can continue to exist without my body and therefore will survive bodily death. I realize that it is more difficult for you to believe in immortality, given your materialism. Perhaps we should focus on our fundamental disagreement about the nature of human minds.

But first I want to be clear: Are you saying that if materialism is true, it is *impossible* to believe in life after death?

MARY: Not really, but immortality becomes very unlikely. I suppose it is still possible; for example, maybe our bodies or just our brains are brought back to life or are duplicated and made to function as before. This would be a way for our minds to persist. But we certainly have no reason to believe that this happens upon bodily death.

DAVE: O.K., but if you believed in God you might think that He does that, and that He transports all of the bodies or brains to some other physical place forever. This is of course not what I believe happens, but it is at least a possible way for a materialist to believe in immortality. It would be based on the idea of bodily resurrection, which obviously has biblical significance.

MARY: Perhaps it is remotely possible, but not very likely. Anyway, it is not what either of us thinks happens to other animals, so why should I think it happens only when human beings die? Also, you are presupposing that God exists in order to perform such miracles, and I have already explained that I am an atheist mainly because I am a materialist. So using God's existence in your reasoning is not very convincing to me.

DAVE: I guess not, but you see my point.

MARY: Of course, but maybe it would be better to discuss in a more direct fashion why you are a dualist and why I am a materialist, since this seems to be the key issue.

DAVE: Sure. Where would you like to start?

MARY: Well, I know of no good arguments for dualism, but there are many good philosophical and scientific reasons favoring materialism.

DAVE: I have a couple of philosophical arguments for dualism, but first let me hear your scientific reasons supporting materialism.

*   *   *   *   *   *   *   *   *   *   *   *

MARY: *First*: Although I suspect that, given your religious views, you do not believe in evolution, I certainly do. And only materialism makes sense in this context.

DAVE: You're right that I am skeptical of evolutionary theory. After all, it really is a somewhat speculative hypothesis, especially compared with other scientific claims. There are many disputes about which evolutionary theory is most valid and even significant disagreement within the scientific community. It is only a theory and we all know how often "science" has been mistaken in the past.

But, anyway, even if evolution occurred in the way you believe, why would materialism follow?

MARY: Well, do you believe that a cat has a mind?

DAVE: Sure.

MARY: How about dogs, lions, and gorillas?

DAVE: Of course, just not minds as advanced as ours.

MARY: Do you believe they survive bodily death? That there is a dog-heaven or a gorilla-heaven? That their minds are distinct nonphysical substances?

DAVE: No to all three questions.

MARY: So then somehow magically we are the only creatures on earth who have a nonphysical substance associated with us? And just how did such an amazing thing happen in the evolutionary process? How and why did nonphysical minds slip into the picture between apes and us?

DAVE: I can't answer that in a purely scientific way, partly because I do not accept that everything must be explained so scientifically.

MARY: O.K., but this brings me to my *second* general reason in favor of materialism. If materialism is true, it is at least possible to explain mental functioning in terms of the brain. On the other hand, if dualism is true, then it would be impossible to observe or to scientifically examine the mind. You must admit that in this sense materialism has a general advantage.

DAVE: Not really. If materialism is true, it does have the advantage in the *scientific* investigation of the mind. But this alone is not a good enough reason to believe that materialism is true.

MARY: Perhaps not, but, together with my earlier point about evolution, it seems rather powerful.

DAVE: I disagree; but do you have another general argument in support of materialism?

MARY: Sure, here is the *third*: You're familiar with the **principle of simplicity** often used in scientific debate.

DAVE: Yes. It says that if there are two theories both of which explain the same number of observations or facts, then we should accept the one that posits fewer objects or the one that is more simple. For example, in astronomy, once we had the alternative theory of elliptical orbits, we came to realize that bizarre and complicated planetary motions were not needed to explain our observations. And there are all kinds of other substances that no longer have any validity for similar reasons; for example, ether.

MARY: Right, and the same goes here. Even assuming *per impossibile* that dualism could explain as much about the mind as materialism, why accept the theory that posits an extra mysterious nonphysical entity when the brain will do just as well? Shouldn't we accept materialism on grounds of simplicity alone?

DAVE: Perhaps, but only within the confines of a scientific debate. The principle of simplicity is, as you mentioned, a scientific principle, and I'm not sure that it should apply to metaphysical issues like the mind-body problem, especially since questions about the soul and immortality are at stake.

MARY: But at least materialists have a chance at scientifically understanding the mind, whereas dualism leaves us with no hope at all.

DAVE: Perhaps, but I find it incredible that the wet, slimy, grey and white stuff in your skull just *is* your mind. You make it sound so obvious, but do you really believe that neurochemical processes in your brain just *are* your thoughts, pains, fears, loves, etc.? You talk about the "magic" of a nonphysical soul. Well, that sounds like just as much magic to me.

MARY: It's not magic or mysterious; it's the very complicated workings of a very complex organ. Any good materialist will admit that he knows comparatively little about how the brain produces conscious mentality, but at least we are learning, whereas dualism offers no hope whatsoever for scientific investigation. The mind is complex, and we should not expect to learn everything about the brain so quickly, but we have made some progress. Give us time and we will have a good scientific explanation of how mental states are constituted by neural states. It may take centuries to establish with any degree of certainty or sense of completion, but we're getting there.

DAVE: I think you are incredibly optimistic. But, more important, you accuse me of having an unfounded faith in immortality and God, whereas you seem to express an equally unfounded faith in scientific knowledge and progress.

MARY: Maybe, but you agreed that animal minds are purely physical and can be identified with their brains. So if a cat's fear that it will be chased by the dog is a purely physical process in the cat's brain, then why do you find it so hard to believe that human mental states are also just brain processes? Granted, we do not currently have all the answers about how the brain accomplishes what it does, but it surely seems reasonable to think that it alone is responsible for mental functioning.

DAVE: Perhaps it all comes back to my theological belief in the soul.

MARY: But you said you wouldn't rely on that for the sake of argument. After all, I explained to you that my main reason for not believing in immortality and God was based precisely on materialism.

DAVE: Fair enough, but I'm convinced there is a deeper problem with materialism regarding just how well it can explain consciousness. But there is an article I want to re-read first. As a matter of fact, this reminds me of Steve, who is very skeptical about materialism, although he is equally doubtful of dualism. He said he was coming tonight, but I presume he was delayed. Oh, but look, there he is now. Hey, Steve, come on over here!

STEVE: Hi Dave. Hi Mary. Sorry I'm late. How are you doing?

MARY: O.K.

DAVE: Fine. We have been discussing philosophy of mind and arguing the case of materialism versus dualism. You know I'm the dualist.

STEVE: Yes, we have had one conversation on the topic. I assume, then, that Mary is the materialist.

MARY: Of course.

STEVE: I remain skeptical of both positions for various reasons. But I don't want to take over the discussion now. How far did you get?

MARY: Well, I think I've finished explaining the various scientific and theoretical advantages of materialism, and I believe that Dave was planning to offer a couple of philosophical arguments for dualism.

STEVE: I'm all ears.

MARY: Me too. Give it your best shot, Dave.

*   *   *   *   *   *   *   *   *   *   *   *   *

DAVE: I can think of many arguments, but I'll restrict myself to two of the more interesting ones. The first is my favorite traditional argument from Descartes, but I need to set it up first.

MARY: Sure.

DAVE: If I could show you that there is a property that the brain has but the mind does not have, or vice versa, wouldn't you both have to accept the conclusion that the mind cannot be identical with the brain?

MARY: I suppose so. Wouldn't that follow from Leibniz's Law?

DAVE: Yes.

STEVE: Wait, what exactly is **Leibniz's Law**?

DAVE: It's a principle about identity which says that "if an object or event x is identical with an object or event y, then x and y have all of the same properties." So if x and y have any different properties, then x cannot be identical with y. The issue is whether we have two different objects or really just two different names which refer to one object.

STEVE: So the issue is whether or not the terms 'mind' and 'brain' refer to the same thing, or whether they name distinct objects. And if one object has a property that the other lacks, then they must be distinct. Therefore, dualism would be true and materialism false.

DAVE: Right. There are of course countless examples of two terms or expressions naming the same thing.

MARY: Yes, like 'heat' and 'mean molecular kinetic energy' or the 'Morning Star' and 'Venus'. The two expressions need not *mean* the same thing, but they *refer* to only one object. This is the way I think of the terms 'mind' and 'brain', or, for example, 'pain' and 'neural state x'. There is really only one object or event.

DAVE: But if one object has a property the other lacks, then they cannot be identical. In your first two examples, Mary, I agree that there is only one thing, but I disagree about the mind. My aim is to show that minds or mental states have properties which brains do not have, or vice versa, and so they are not identical.

MARY: Well, what property do you think can demonstrate this?

DAVE: Divisibility. To paraphrase Descartes: My body is divisible, since it can be separated, e.g. my arm or my finger can be cut off; my brain can be cut in half. In short, my body has parts. On the other hand, when I think to myself about my mind, I cannot understand the idea that my mind is divisible. I can't understand my mind 'split' in any way analogous to my body. Can I understand my current thought divided, say, in half? No. Does it have a left half and a right half? Of course not. So the mind must be distinct from the brain. The latter has a property, divisibility, which the former lacks.

Maybe we should put it more formally so we can more easily keep it in mind. Let's call it the **Divisibility Argument**:

(1) My body, which includes my brain, is divisible.
(2) I cannot conceive of my mind as divisible.
Therefore, (3) My mind is distinct from any part of my body.

STEVE: In premise 2, aren't you just assuming that the mind is non-physical? This would be **begging the question**: assuming what you are trying to prove, namely, that dualism is true. After all, if materialism is true, then my mind can be divided in the same way that any part of my body can be.

DAVE: No. I'm not begging the question. I'm just reporting something that seems obvious when I introspect, namely, that my mind is not divisible.

MARY: O.K., but there is something odd about the term 'divisible'. If you mean 'can be split up', then you might be begging the question against the materialist. So I assume you mean something more like 'has parts'?

DAVE: Yes, and I believe that is closer to Descartes' original meaning. So now what's the problem?

MARY: Well, even when I introspect to myself about my mind, I think I can understand it as having parts, and so premise 2 would be false. It has parts such as my memories, my beliefs, my fears, my desires, etc. In short, I think of my mind as having compartments containing different types of mental states. They are the parts which compose my mind. If my mind is a bundle of mental states, then the mental states are the parts. Why isn't that "conceiving of my mind as divisible"?

DAVE: But aren't you now begging the question? That is, assuming materialism to be true?

MARY: I don't think so. What I said does not presuppose either position. If anything, you are assuming dualism by assuming that a nonphysical thing cannot have parts.

DAVE: Again, for the reason given earlier, I don't think so.

STEVE: But, Mary, I recall Descartes having said something in reply to your claim that you can conceive of your mind as divisible, that is, as having parts or compartments such as beliefs, desires, and so on.

MARY: What was it?

STEVE: Descartes claimed that different mental faculties cannot truly be thought of as the mind's parts, because it is the *same mind* which employs itself in willing, desiring, believing, understanding, and so on. What do you say to that?

MARY: Well, this assumes the troublesome picture of the mind as some kind of enduring unified entity that exists mysteriously behind the scenes and that observes each mental state as it occurs. There are good reasons not to think of the mind in such a peculiar way. For one thing, my mind is not something *in addition to* the sequence of my mental states, but rather is simply the entity which *is composed of* my mental states. Descartes makes it sound as though the mind views the sequence of our mental states in the way that we view segments of film in a continuous movie. But this is difficult to understand. Your mind is not something extra behind the scenes passively watching the train of your mental states. It is composed of parts whether or not we introspect it that way.

STEVE: I know what you mean; I was just curious about how you might respond.

MARY: O.K., but, anyway, I have trouble overall with Dave's use of the term 'conceive'.

DAVE: How so?

MARY: As even Descartes recognized, the term 'conceive' might mean either 'imagine' or 'understand'. Imagining literally involves 'forming an image of' or 'picturing' in one's mind, whereas understanding is more 'conceptual' and does not require the ability to picture something. So when you say you cannot conceive of your mind as divisible, which do you mean?

DAVE: Why does that matter?

MARY: Because, first, if you mean 'imagine', then you are in deep trouble.

DAVE: Why?

MARY: You would be implicitly assuming in premise 2 that since you cannot imagine something to be the case, then it could not be the case. Since you cannot imagine your mind as divisible, then your mind cannot be divisible. But inferring *from* the fact that something is unimaginable *to* the fact that it is not the case or not possible is a terrible inference.

I'll give you an example: I cannot imagine a five-hundred-sided figure, but it clearly does not follow that there isn't one, let alone that one is not possible. Of course, I can still 'understand' or 'conceive' what such a figure would be like. Perhaps I could even draw one with the help of an artist. The same goes for imagining a leopard with forty-five spots, picturing two billion dollars in my apartment, being ninty-three million miles away from the sun, etc.

DAVE: I see. Well, I probably should then mean by 'conceive' something more like 'understand'. If we cannot understand something in the sense that it is conceptually incoherent, like a 'round square', then it wouldn't be possible. This is the way I think of the term 'conceive' in premise 2. I can't understand predicating 'divisibility' to my mind or my mental states when I introspect.

STEVE: But *we* seem to be able to understand that. Remember Mary's point about thinking of her mind as having parts, etc. This seems to go against your claim. Maybe you just don't have the same ability to understand as we do.

MARY: Exactly, Steve.

DAVE: Let's not start attacking my intelligence. Anyway, even if I grant your point here, it wouldn't alter the idea that individual mental states are not divisible, and so the argument could be recast by emphasizing the fact that I cannot conceive of my individual mental states as having parts.

STEVE: But if that is done, then the same seems true about individual physical particles. That is, it is just as difficult to understand that every physical particle is divisible. Many philosophers and physicists believe that ultimately there must be physical particles without parts. So you cannot use the appropriate difference between mental states and all physical stuff in order to prove your conclusion.

Dave: Perhaps, but, according to your materialism, Mary, wouldn't an individual mental state involve more than a single particle in the brain?

Mary: Of course. Well, anyway, there is another serious problem with the whole way that you approach this issue. It has to do with how you emphasize the first-person or 'introspective' point of view.

Dave: How do you mean?

Mary: Well, we can learn about our minds by thinking to ourselves, but surely we can also learn many things from a third-person point of view. That is, you can learn things about my mind and I can learn things about your mind through observation. Scientifically speaking, psychiatrists and neuropsychologists can by observation discover quite a bit about the workings of another's mind. Don't you agree?

Dave: Yes, as long as you are not assuming that the brain is the mind.

Mary: No, but third-person observation is important in the investigation of the mind, isn't it?

Dave: Again, yes, we can infer things about another's mind on the basis of observation; so what's your point?

Mary: Your method in the Divisibility Argument assumes that the true nature of the mind can be grasped solely through introspection or from the first-person point of view. And this is wrong, as even you seem to agree.

Dave: How so? And what does this have to do with the Divisibility Argument?

Mary: Even if I grant you that *I* cannot conceive of *my* mind as divided, this would only be so from the first-person perspective. It would not follow that my mind is not really divisible or could not be conceived as such from another's perspective. Even if *I* cannot conceive of *my* mind as divided from *my* point of view, it doesn't follow that *you* cannot understand *my* mind as divided.

STEVE: Right, and also, Dave, you seem to be making a general claim about the nature of all minds, i.e. that they all are nonphysical and distinct from their corresponding bodies. You are ultimately not making a claim just about the nature of your own mind. But I don't see what entitles you to make such a general claim.

DAVE: It is difficult to see how anyone could say that another's mind is divisible without assuming that materialism is true. Aren't you saying that a scientist can view your brain as having parts and so therefore your mind is divisible?

MARY: No, I don't think I am assuming materialism. Imagine someone who knows nothing about philosophy or about the brain, and has not thought about this issue at all. Doesn't it make sense for him to say to a friend: "There are parts of your mind that are hidden from me," "There are parts of your mind and personality which I don't understand," etc.?

STEVE: Actually, what about multiple personality disorder? Take a severe case where a person, Joe, rarely even realizes that he has the problem. We can and do see Joe's mind as divided even if he doesn't think of himself that way. We learn about Joe's condition through third-person observation and eventually through scientific investigation.

MARY: Good! Right! And we certainly aren't assuming materialism when we make this judgment about Joe's mind. Moreover, this is a clear case where the third-person perspective reveals the true nature of a mind as divided regardless of how it seems from the first-person perspective. So your argument fails here as well.

DAVE: Interesting, but in multiple personality cases I'd be tempted to believe that the subject really has two minds rather than one divided mind. Neither mind is divisible.

MARY: Are you serious?

DAVE: Yes. Think about something we often say: "He is an entirely different person from yesterday," etc. If, as seems obvious, different people have different minds, then we should say that two different minds are associated with Joe's body.

MARY: But surely such talk is merely metaphorical; we don't mean literally that such a person really has two distinct minds.

DAVE: Perhaps. I'm not sure.

STEVE: Oh, come on! You do see the obvious problems: If Joe has two minds, why don't we all "really" have two or more minds? If Joe really has two minds, then which one does the name 'Joe' refer to? If a multiple personality has five personalities, then does he or she have five minds?

MARY: And how about the less dramatic example of an amnesia victim? Isn't it literally true to say that some parts of that person's mind are hidden from him and from us?

DAVE: Let me think about that one. But I understand that some well-respected philosophers and psychologists agree with me on the question of two minds.

MARY: But don't they usually have materialist reasons for their position? For example, reasons which have to do with the two hemispheres in the brain?

DAVE: I'll have to find out.

STEVE: Actually, Mary, let Dave off the hook on this one because I'm eager to hear his other favorite argument for dualism. You said earlier that the Divisibility Argument was only one of two.

*   *   *   *   *   *   *   *   *   *   *   *

DAVE: Yes. Here it is:

(1) Mental states are knowable through introspection.
(2) Brain states are *not* knowable through introspection.
Therefore, (3) Mental states are not brain states.

Let's call this the **Argument from Introspection**. It also relies on Leibniz's Law and uses a different property to prove the distinctness of brain states and mental states: the property of being knowable through introspection. In this case, the mind has the property and the brain lacks it. I can know about my feelings and thoughts by introspection, but clearly I cannot learn anything about my brain through introspection. So my mental states cannot *be* my brain states. After all, humans were around a long time before we knew anything about our brains, but it would be ridiculous to say that we didn't know anything about our minds during that time.

STEVE: Can you give a particular example?

DAVE: Sure. Right now I have a desire for another drink. I know that I have that mental state simply by examining my own mind and without knowing anything about what might "correspond" to it in terms of brain activity. Thus, my desire cannot simply *be* the brain process, as you seem to believe.

MARY: *First* of all, you are making a mistake similar to the one you made earlier, in that you rely heavily on introspection.

DAVE: How so?

MARY: Before I explain, let me give an analogy with our perception of outer objects. When we look at a physical object, do we perceive its true nature?

DAVE: I suppose not if you mean in the scientific sense of ultimate particles, not to mention the difficult issue of color. We learn about the object's true physical make-up through scientific investigation.

MARY: And there is of course a very good reason why we are not built to perceive the world in that way.

STEVE: I'd say. It would be very confusing if all we perceived were atoms whizzing around. Our species wouldn't have survived.

MARY: Right. And so why shouldn't the same go for mental states, which are the objects of *inner* perception?

DAVE: How do you mean?

MARY: Well, you perceive your desire for a drink via introspection, but there is no reason to suppose that its true nature is revealed that way. When we perceive the table we do not perceive its true nature without further scientific study. But this doesn't mean that the table is entirely distinct from the atoms that compose it, right?

DAVE: Right.

MARY: So, similarly, just because you do not perceive your desire *as a brain state*, it does not follow that it is distinct from your brain. In other words, the Argument from Introspection fails to prove that mental states are distinct from brain states. It's merely that we cannot learn about any identity through introspection. But ignorance about the true nature of mental states cannot be used as an argument for dualism.

STEVE: Right, and just as before with outer objects, that's what we should expect because it would be ridiculous if we did introspect electro-chemical reactions when we focused our attention on our mental states. Talk about confusing! I have a hard enough time concentrating on a problem as it is! We are fortunately aware of our mental states only *as mental states* and not *as brain states*, but it doesn't follow that they are distinct. Objects are not always really the way they appear, and this goes as much for inner mental states as it does for outer reality.

DAVE: I suppose so, but at most you've only shown that mental states *could* be brain states, nothing stronger.

MARY: But that's all I need for now. My aim here has only been to refute the Argument from Introspection. Other independent support for materialism has already been given. But, anyway, there is a *second* and more serious objection to your argument.

DAVE: What's that?

MARY: It has to do with your application of Leibniz's Law. I have recently learned that the Law cannot be used in contexts like this one.

DAVE: What kinds of contexts?

MARY: Leibniz's Law fails in what are called **intensional contexts**, i.e. cases where replacing one co-referring term with another can change a statement's truth-value.

STEVE: I'm not sure I follow.

MARY: Let me explain. Remember how two different expressions or terms can refer to the same object?

STEVE: Yes, like 'heat' and 'mean molecular kinetic energy' or 'Babe Ruth' and 'the first baseball player to hit 60 home runs in a season' or 'water' and 'H_2O'.

MARY: Right. These are called 'co-referring' terms or expressions.

DAVE: So?

MARY: Well, normally when one of the expressions is replaced by the other in a sentence, the new sentence retains the same truth-value. That is, if the first sentence was false, then it remains false; if it was true, it stays true.

DAVE: O.K. So, for example, the following sentence is true:

(1) Babe Ruth played most of his career for the New York Yankees.

Now replace 'Babe Ruth' with the other expression and we get:

(2) The first baseball player to hit 60 home runs in a season played most of his career for the New York Yankees.

Sentence (2) is also true. I can see how these can be generated *ad infinitum*.

STEVE: Me too, and also for false sentences remaining false after the substitution of a co-referring expression. For example, it is false that "Babe Ruth weighed 140 pounds in his last playing year"; and so it remains false that "The first baseball player to hit 60 home runs in a season weighed 140 pounds in his last playing year."

MARY: Right! And these are the kinds of cases where Leibniz's Law *can be* used. That is, we would expect to find any property true of Babe Ruth to be true of the first player to hit 60 home runs, and anything false to remain false.

Suppose you were reading a history book and you wondered whether two of the persons mentioned weren't really the same person even though two different names had been used. In order to show non-identity, all you needed was to find a single property that one had and the other lacked.

DAVE: Yes, and that's what I've done in Argument from Introspection.

MARY: But the problem is that in some contexts the truth-value will change after the substitution, and so Leibniz's Law cannot be used to prove non-identity. One such context involves sentences with mental expressions like 'believes that', 'conceives that', thinks that', 'knows that', etc. Otherwise, we could prove the non-identity of anything that has two names or expressions for it.

STEVE: Can you give an example?

MARY: Sure. My sister Jane knows very little about baseball, but does know that Babe Ruth played primarily for the Yankees. Jane knows that he was a great player but knows few, if any, statistics. Take the sentence

(3) Jane knows that Babe Ruth played most of his career for the Yankees.

This statement is true, but now make the substitution, and we have the following *false* sentence:

(4) Jane knows that the first player to hit 60 home runs in a season played most of his career for the Yankees.

STEVE: I see. Here's another one: My four-year-old niece, Karen, knows nothing about chemistry, but knows what water is. The following is true:

(5) Karen knows that her pool is filled with water.

But it is false that:

(6) Karen knows that her pool is filled with H_2O.

DAVE: I see, but what does all this have to do with the Argument from Introspection?

MARY: I'm getting there. But do you see how if we used Leibniz's Law in this context we could, for example, prove that water is not identical with H_2O?

DAVE: I think so, but explain.

STEVE: Let me give it a try.

MARY: O.K.

STEVE: Water has a property which H_2O lacks, namely, "known by Karen to be in her pool." Therefore, by Leibniz's Law, water is not identical with H_2O.

MARY: Do you see how the same problem always haunts Leibniz's Law in these contexts?

DAVE: I guess so.

MARY: Well, then, the problem with the Argument from Introspection is that it applies Leibniz's Law where it shouldn't, namely, in an intensional context. So you have not shown that mental states are distinct from brain states any more than we have just shown water to be distinct from H_2O.

Just as Karen is ignorant of H_2O and has to learn about its identity with water through science, so are we often ignorant about which brain states correspond to our mental states. But we can learn about them through the scientific discipline known as neurophysiology. In neither case, however, is any non-identity shown. You simply can't use properties like 'knowable through introspection' to show non-identity.

STEVE: Right. And again, if Leibniz's Law could be used in such contexts, then we could show non-identity in any situation. All we'd have to do is find someone who knows, thinks, or believes one thing about an object while being ignorant about some other aspect of it.

MARY: So my current desire to have another drink can still be identical with one of my brain processes, even though I couldn't know it through introspection.

DAVE: I see the problem. Perhaps it is insurmountable, but you talk as if you do know that mental states are brain states.

MARY: I think I do. At the least, it seems a much more rational belief than dualism.

STEVE: But isn't Dave right to question your optimism about materialism? You speak of "correlations" between mental states and brain processes. That seems rather weak as evidence for materialism.

MARY: I disagree. You have to take it as only one piece of evidence for materialism, along with evolution and the other considerations I had discussed with Dave before you came.

STEVE: I know what you mean. Remember, we also talked about it last week.

MARY: Yes, I remember. You must admit that we have a good deal of knowledge about the way neurons work and how some brain activity is correlated with certain types of mental states. For example, many parts of the brain are clearly linked to pain, memories, and visual experiences.

DAVE: I'm not sure what these correlations prove about the nature of the mind. Anyway, neuroscientists don't have a clue about most higher-order cognitive functioning.

MARY: I'm not saying we have all the answers now. Far from it. But at least we're progressing; we're learning more and more every day. On the other hand, if you are right, Dave, then we couldn't scientifically learn anything about the mind, since it is not physical and therefore could not be the object of any scientific investigation. I don't see how you could opt for such a theory.

DAVE: Well, first, I have nothing against scientifically examining and learning about the brain. It is no doubt a very important part of the body. But I do not believe that my mind *is* my brain, or that my current desire for another drink and my love for my wife *just are* some electro-chemical processes in my brain. Second, I do not share your apparent desire to restrict reality to the physical.

MARY: I am not arbitrarily opposed to the existence of nonphysical things, but I fail to see the basis for believing in nonphysical minds in this particular case. I believe in other nonphysical entities.

STEVE: Like what? Not God, right? That's what you told me the other day.

MARY: I do not believe in God, but I believe in numbers. Numbers must be nonphysical entities.

STEVE: Why?

MARY: Well, for example, we couldn't go find the number 5 itself and destroy it. Even if a mad scientist found a way to destroy every instance of 5, would the number *itself* have gone of existence?

STEVE: No.

MARY: And if the existing 5's were all destroyed, would the first person who wrote '5' have created it anew?

STEVE: No, so I suppose the number 5 itself and all other numbers have always existed and always will. Numbers are nonphysical and eternal.

MARY: There are certainly some numbers which have never been written down anywhere. Don't they exist now? Of course. Would they only come into existence after they were written down? No. Numbers are nonphysical and eternal.

DAVE: I'm glad to hear you say that, so why don't you give non-physical minds the same due?

MARY: Because I don't have any reason to. Besides, there are other serious problems with dualism that we haven't discussed yet.

DAVE: Like what?

MARY: Well, let's meet again tomorrow. All this talk about a desire for another drink has made me thirsty. Let's go play some pool and talk about something else.

STEVE: Sounds good. I was starting to lose my mind or brain or whatever.

DAVE: O.K. Let's pick it up here tomorrow.

THE SECOND NIGHT

MARY: Hi Steve. You're right on time.

STEVE: Well, I'm ready to go. I have many questions for both of you. Where's Dave?

MARY: He should be here soon.

STEVE: Here he comes.

MARY: How are you doing, Dave? Are you ready for more of this?

DAVE: You bet. But where did we leave off last night?

STEVE: I remember. Mary was saying that she had other serious objections to dualism.

DAVE: Well, fire away, Mary.

STEVE: And I have some real problems with dualism regarding the interaction between the mind and the body. But go ahead, Mary.

MARY: Actually, my main problem with dualism has to do with that too.

DAVE: Well?

MARY: Let me first explain another obvious advantage of materialism and then get to the objection to dualism. First, you must agree that mental states causally interact with the body or the brain, and vice versa.

DAVE: Of course, and virtually all dualists agree. This dualist position is called **interactionism**.

MARY: For example, if I kick you in the leg, Dave, eventually you will experience a mental state of pain. Your pain, in turn, might cause your heart to beat faster, or might even cause you to kick me in return.

STEVE: And, as we know from last night, a desire for a drink will cause my body to move to buy a beer. And, conversely, we also know that bodily behavior can cause mental changes, sometimes very severe and damaging. The examples could go on forever.

MARY: There is no conceptual bar to materialism explaining such causal interaction between the mind and body or brain. I'm not saying that we know all of the details yet, but we do know a lot about how the nervous system and brain work. So, for example, kicking you in the leg causes damage to a particular area and the nerves cause an impulse and message to travel up through the spinal column. Ultimately, the impulse will reach an area of the brain, and the final neural firing in the sequence *is* the pain you feel. Conversely, we know how some mental states (e.g. anger) cause bodily changes and certain bodily movements.

DAVE: A nice story, but I must disagree with your identification of the pain and the neural firing.

MARY: But the point is that materialism at least has the potential to explain the obvious causation which occurs between the mind and the body. Since the mind is part of the body, then there is nothing inherently bizarre about such interaction. There is causation within the physical world, and now it's up to us to explain it as best we can through further scientific investigation.

DAVE: But I do not think that the pain or anger *just is* one of the brain states in the chain of causes. Mental states are not physical entities; rather they occur within our nonphysical minds.

STEVE: I think Mary's point is that materialism at least has a chance at explaining the causal interaction between the mind and the body, whereas dualism has none. Therefore, we should accept the more explanatorily useful theory.

MARY: Exactly.

DAVE: But what's your specific objection?

STEVE: Well, there are two major objections to interactionism as far as I know. *One* has to do with the general problem of explaining how physical events can cause events in a nonphysical mind, and vice versa. First of all, one side of the causal interaction will always be unobservable, so how could any dualist explanation be forthcoming?

MARY: Dave, take my example from earlier. I kick you in the leg and you then must acknowledge the physical facts about what happens up through the nervous system and into the brain. But instead of simply admitting that the last neural firing in the causal sequence *just is* the pain you feel, you seem to think that the last neural firing *causes* the further pain state in your nonphysical mind.

DAVE: Right. The mental state is not identical with the neural state, but rather is caused by it.

MARY: But how in the world does that happen?

DAVE: I don't know, but that doesn't mean it doesn't happen that way.

STEVE: Doesn't that bother you, Dave? Why believe that causation could even exist between such radically different substances?

DAVE: I don't have the answer, but neither do you.

MARY: Sure, but at least we have a chance to explain mental-physical interaction. If dualism were true, then it would be impossible to explain or understand it. Doesn't that bother you?

DAVE: Sometimes, but I obviously don't share your craving to have everything explained by science. We also all know how often science has been mistaken in the past, and I don't see why I should become a materialist just because materialism seems more consistent with science.

STEVE: Actually, I'm convinced that science, and especially neurophysiology, could go some way toward resolving the issue between dualism and materialism. That is, there is an experiment that could help determine which view is right.

MARY: Really? What?

STEVE: We have been talking about brain states causing mental states. Let's look at it the other way around. Dualism also has the converse problem: how do nonphysical mental events cause brain changes and eventually bodily movements?

MARY: Of course.

STEVE: So now if dualism were true, we should expect to see

neurons regularly firing without any physical cause. Right?

DAVE: I'm not sure I follow.

STEVE: Well, according to materialism, the brain is a closed physical system, and we know from neurology how neurons cause each other to fire. I'll skip over the details here. If materialism is true, then whenever a neuron fires, the cause must be some other physical or neural state.

DAVE: Right.

STEVE: But if dualism is true, neural activity must often be caused by nonphysical mental events. Right?

DAVE: I suppose so.

STEVE: But there has never been any evidence to suggest that this is so. That is, we do not find neurons regularly firing without any other physical cause. So interactionist dualism must be false.

DAVE: Are you sure there is no evidence favoring the dualist?

STEVE: Not as far as I know.

DAVE: Now that you mention it, I thought I heard one of the other graduate students say that he knows of a few scientists who have become dualists for this very reason. I wasn't sure what he meant then, but now I see the point. That is, perhaps the jury is still out in the scientific community regarding the evidence.

MARY: Really? I'd be interested in learning more about this, but I'd be shocked to learn that neurons fired regularly without any physical cause. However, I agree that if this were so, then that would be good evidence, and even scientific evidence, for substance dualism.

STEVE: Maybe we should look into this a bit more. But I am still baffled about exactly how any dualist interaction could take place, and that is one reason why I often lean toward materialism.

DAVE: What's the other reason? You said earlier you had two.

STEVE: Right. The *second* serious problem has to do with the fact that dualist interactionism is inconsistent with the well-established scientific **Principle of the Conservation of Energy**, which says that the total amount of energy in the universe, or any controlled part of it, remains constant. So any loss of energy in a cause must be passed on as a corresponding gain of energy in the effect. The cue ball loses energy when it hits another ball, but the energy does not magically disappear and go out of existence; it is passed on to the other ball. In general, then, energy is neither created nor destroyed.

DAVE: So where's the contradiction?

STEVE: Interactionism claims that there is causation between the physical world and the nonphysical mental realm.

DAVE: Yes.

STEVE: But since minds would not be part of the physical world, there would then be sudden gains and losses in the amount of total energy whenever mental events caused physical events or vice versa. That is, when a physical event caused a mental event, energy would literally go out of the physical world, since causation involves a transfer of energy from cause to effect. Conversely, when a mental event caused a physical event, there would have to be a gain of energy in the physical world.

MARY: Yes. This is a serious problem for you, Dave. Clearly there is no scientific evidence of such a bizarre phenomenon.

DAVE: Well, have controlled experiments been performed using thinking people enclosed in an area in order to determine whether there are any such gains or losses?

MARY: I'm not sure. Such experiments may not be so easy to perform because it would be difficult for physicists to measure what would have to be very small violations of the Principle. But even assuming that they can be performed accurately, you can't believe that such losses or gains would actually occur.

DAVE: Maybe they would. For someone who relies so heavily on science, Mary, you really aren't sure about many potentially important scientific experiments.

MARY: But the fact remains that dualism is inconsistent with the Conservation of Energy Principle. One says that the amount of energy remains constant and the other entails that there are losses and gains of energy. If we made a graph with "amount of energy" on the vertical and "time" on the horizontal, the Conservation Principle would yield a straight line across. Where it began on the horizontal line would depend on which enclosed portion of the world is measured. On the other hand, substance dualism would yield a line going across and often up and down, with the amount of energy varying whenever mental-physical causation occurred. Clearly both can't be true, and, given a choice between them, why would anyone opt for dualism?

STEVE: I certainly wouldn't.

DAVE: Well, maybe the Conservation of Energy Principle isn't true, or is only true concerning purely physical objects without minds.

MARY: Are you serious? The Principle is true everywhere in the entire universe, including among all other animals, but then does *not* apply *only* when humans are involved? Incredible!

DAVE: Maybe, but I'm simply not as inclined to treat the Principle as so certain. For one thing, it is obviously an inductive generalization from a relatively small sample of experiments. Clearly, astronomers and physicists cannot be certain that it holds everywhere in the entire vast universe.

MARY: Well, what can I say? I still don't see why anyone would give more weight to dualism.

DAVE: I do not have the confidence in science that you do. Plus, there are other possible explanations consistent with dualism.

STEVE: Like what?

DAVE: You mentioned the "transfer of energy from the cause to the effect," and you have simply assumed it in your argument.

STEVE: Of course; that's the way it works.

DAVE: No. That's the way it works *as far as we know in the physical world*. Maybe it does not always work that way. Or maybe causation between the physical and the nonphysical does not involve a transfer of energy in the same way. After all, you'd expect it to be a bit different, wouldn't you?

So even if the level of energy does remain constant, as the Conservation Principle says, that may not really contradict interactionism. You must remember that it is a principle of physics, which means that it may apply only in the physical world. Things may work quite differently with mental-physical interaction.

MARY: Your faith in these unfounded speculations never ceases to amaze me.

DAVE: Well, your faith and optimism about science are often just as unfounded.

MARY: I really don't see how you could compare.

*   *   *   *   *   *   *   *   *   *   *   *

STEVE: I have to agree with Mary on this point. But also, Dave, don't you think that brain damage causing mental defects refutes dualism?

DAVE: No. Why would you think that?

STEVE: We know that damage to certain specific brain areas causes specific mental problems, e.g. memory loss, visual and hearing problems, and language comprehension disorders.

MARY: Yes, and doesn't it follow that those brain areas just *were* where the mental states occurred? That is, doesn't such evidence show materialism to be true, and therefore dualism false?

DAVE: Of course not.

STEVE: Why?

DAVE: Because if you damage or eliminate a cause, then you damage or eliminate the effect.

MARY: How do you mean?

DAVE: You recall that interactionism acknowledges, for example, that brain events cause mental events.

MARY: Sure, and you deny that the brain event (BE) *is* the mental event (ME).

DAVE: Well, brain damage cannot show dualism to be false, because if part of the causal sequence of events to one's nonphysical mind is disturbed or damaged, then we should expect there to be a corresponding problem in the mind. I claim that "BE causes ME," whereas you insist that "BE = ME." But in either case damage to the brain area will result in damage to the correlated mental state. Obviously, if your materialism is true, then damage to the brain area will result in damage to the mind because you believe that the BEs *are* MEs.

MARY: Right.

DAVE: But interactionism can equally well explain this phenomenon. If BE causes ME, then, when the relevant brain area is damaged, the corresponding part of the mind is also disturbed, because the cause of ME has been disturbed or destroyed. So you can't use brain damage to refute interactionism or to support materialism. If, for example, there is damage to the brain area which typically *causes* conscious visual experiences, then I can just as easily explain why the person's visual capacities have been damaged.

STEVE: Interesting.

MARY: Perhaps you can squirm out of this one, Dave, but you still face the two devastating problems from earlier.

And I'm not so sure that your reply really helps you in the end. Doesn't it cause trouble in terms of your belief in immortality?

DAVE: How so?

MARY: Well, take the case where brain damage causes the destruction or elimination of a conscious mental capacity.

DAVE: Yes.

MARY: Now, what happens to the brain upon bodily death?

STEVE: The entire brain ceases to function and is ultimately destroyed through decomposition.

DAVE: Right.

MARY: Well, by your own reasoning, Dave, interactionism would have to admit that when the brain is eliminated or destroyed, the mind is also eliminated or destroyed. That is, the cause of your mind is destroyed and therefore so is the effect. Thus, there could not be immortality because one's mind would cease to exist upon brain death. So what is the point of your reply here if it undermines your belief in immortality? I mean, that's how we started all this last night. Remember?

DAVE: Sure, but I'm not convinced that my belief in immortality is seriously threatened.

MARY: Why not? You might still want to believe that your mind is a nonphysical substance distinct from your body, but if it causally depends for its existence on the proper functioning of your brain, then there cannot be any immortality.

STEVE: Interesting point. Isn't this a serious problem for you, Dave?

DAVE: Perhaps, but maybe the mind only causally depends on the brain during the time our bodies are functioning on earth. And then, after bodily death, one's mind no longer depends on one's brain to function properly. My mind might just causally depend on my brain here and now, but it need not depend for its existence on anything else after bodily death.

STEVE: I'm not convinced by that, Dave. It really sounds rather arbitrary to concede that your mind depends on your brain up until bodily death, but then to claim that it suddenly doesn't depend on anything else after that point.

MARY: Sounds weak and arbitrary to me too. Also, what happens to those destroyed conscious capacities upon bodily death?

DAVE: What do you mean?

MARY: Well, suppose you have severe amnesia during the last few years of your life, caused by brain damage. Wouldn't that mental damage then carry over to your "afterlife"?

If so, then the mind's causal dependence on the brain has some very serious and disturbing consequences for the quality of one's afterlife. Even if your mind is able to survive brain death, what kind of mind would it be?

On the other hand, *if* any or all mental damage does *not* carry over to the afterlife, then you really need to explain how the mental damage one suffers during life on earth magically disappears upon bodily death. I mean, how is all this mental functioning suddenly recovered or restored?

DAVE: I see the dilemma. I'll need to think about it. You raise a whole new issue concerning the nature of the afterlife.

*   *   *   *   *   *   *   *   *   *   *   *

STEVE: Perhaps there are other versions of dualism that can avoid some of Dave's problems, but I do not know of any.

DAVE: Well, there is another type of dualism that avoids most of the problems facing interactionism.

STEVE: What is it?

DAVE: It's called **parallelism**. It is a form of dualism because it holds that the mind is a nonphysical substance distinct from the body. But it denies that the two causally interact, and therefore it avoids the problems which stem from any alleged mind-body causal interaction.

STEVE: But what does parallelism say about the mind-body relationship? Surely it must give some explanation.

DAVE: Yes, parallelism says that mental events and bodily events are correlated, but that there is no interaction between the mental and physical realms. So physical events cause other physical events, and mental events cause other mental events.

STEVE: In other words, my mental realm runs parallel to the sequence of my bodily, and especially brain, events in some kind of perfect synchrony or harmony.

DAVE: Right. The idea is that the mental and physical realms operate along parallel tracks, always in perfect harmony. So, for example, when I kick you in the leg and then you feel pain, there is no causation between those events, but rather your mental "track" is such that you feel the pain at about the same time as the physical bodily event occurs. And the same type of answer goes for other familiar examples of alleged mind-body interaction.

STEVE: So I have a mental sequence of events and a bodily sequence of events running in parallel to each other without any causal interaction at all between them?

DAVE: Yes. Think of it as follows:

$$ME1 \rightarrow ME2 \rightarrow ME3 \rightarrow ME4 \rightarrow ME5 \rightarrow ME6 \text{ and so on.}$$
$$BE1 \rightarrow BE2 \rightarrow BE3 \rightarrow BE4 \rightarrow BE5 \rightarrow BE6 \text{ and so on.}$$

Mental Event$_1$ causes Mental Event$_2$ and so on. Bodily Event$_1$ causes Bodily Event$_2$ and so on. But there is no causation going from the mental to the physical, or vice versa. BE1 might be the leg damage or injury from my kick and ME1 might be the pain you feel. They occur almost simultaneously, but BE1 does not cause ME1.

MARY: I think Leibniz used the analogy of two clocks or watches that are in perfect agreement. They have been constructed in such a way that their subsequent agreement is guaranteed. Think of the mind and body this way. That is, they reliably correspond to each other in the way that perfectly synchronized clocks correspond. Minds follow their own laws of development, and bodies follow the laws of physics and motion.

STEVE: I see. Granted that this alternative form of dualism avoids the problems with interactionism, doesn't it suffer from other and even more serious difficulties?

DAVE: I think so. That's why I opt for interactionism.

STEVE: Why exactly aren't you a parallelist?

DAVE: My main reason is simply that I do not wish to deny the apparently obvious fact that mental events cause bodily events, and vice versa. Remember all of the examples we used earlier?

STEVE: Sure.

DAVE: I mean, the parallelist seems committed to holding that statements like "your kick to my leg caused my pain" are literally false. I can't accept that. Just think of all of the false statements we would be making all the time. I prefer not to stray so far from common sense.

STEVE: I see. Statements like "my looking at the carpet caused me to have a red visual experience," "my eating the steak caused me to have a certain taste sensation," "my desire for a drink caused me to move toward the bar," and "your talking to me caused me to have certain auditory sensations" would all literally be false according to parallelism.

DAVE: Yes, because there really is no mental-physical interaction at all. That's a bit too much for me to swallow. I can't believe that we could be so wrong about the truth of such statements.

MARY: Parallelism does sound very counterintuitive when you put it that way. Of course, we can agree that physical events cause other physical events. And we can agree that mental events *sometimes* cause other mental events, e.g. my thought about the escaped convict causes me to have a fear for my life. But to deny all mind-body interaction seems wrong.

DAVE: I agree with you there. Think about the kick and the pain again. Let's say that you were watching television just before I kicked you. You then felt the pain. We would all say that your pain was caused by my kick to your leg. But it seems that the parallelist must say that your pain was not caused by my kick to your leg, but rather was caused by your immediately prior mental state involving a visual experience of the television. This sounds absurd to me.

And if the pain is not caused by the previous mental state, then how or why did it arise at that time? Was it just a lucky coincidence?

MARY: Good point. Here is another related objection to parallelism. What causes your first mental state when you wake up in the morning? I set my alarm to wake me up with radio music. Let's say that I wake up to a Rolling Stones song so that my first conscious mental state of the day is an auditory experience. What caused it? We would all answer with an explanation about sound waves, ears, and neural firings, although we might have some disagreement about the true nature of the mental state.

But the parallelist would have to say that my previous mental state caused the auditory experience. That's very strange. How, for example, could my last thought from the previous night have caused this auditory experience eight hours later?

STEVE: That is rather bizarre, especially since there would probably be no logical connection between the two mental states. I mean, your last thought of the previous night might have been about calling your mother today. How or why would that cause an auditory experience of a Rolling Stones song?

DAVE: Exactly, and so I'd prefer to accept the obvious fact of mind-body interaction and deal with the objections to interactionism as I did earlier. Parallelism can avoid those objections, but the price is much too high.

MARY: Here is another objection to parallelism. We might ask the question: Why does the synchrony hold between the mental and the physical? I mean, the parallelist shouldn't just announce that it exists without any reason. He or she must explain why it occurs. It can't just be some continuous lucky accident. What keeps the mental and physical realms from getting "out of synch"?

DAVE: Well, the answer will likely come with the help of the clock analogy.

MARY: O.K., but who or what sets our mental and physical clocks so that they always run perfectly together? What prevents the "tracks" from sometimes looking like this:

$$ME5 \rightarrow ME6 \rightarrow ME7 \rightarrow ME8$$
$$BE5 \rightarrow BE6 \rightarrow BE7 \rightarrow BE8 \rightarrow BE9?$$

DAVE: The parallelist will probably say that the only answer is God. Only God could have the knowledge and power to engineer things so perfectly. God sets our mental and body clocks perfectly. Otherwise, for example, I might sometimes feel the pain in my leg *before* you kick me.

MARY: Oh, come on! I can't believe that such a dualist must embrace theism in order to defend her solution to the mind-body problem, especially after our conversation early last night. It just seems backwards to me.

The main reason I do not believe in God has to do with my belief in materialism, which leads me, in turn, not to believe in immortality. Here we have a dualist view which can help us to understand the possibility of immortality, but in order to handle a very basic objection it assumes that God exists. What more can I say? That type of reasoning is not very convincing to me.

STEVE: I agree, but there would be another serious objection to parallelism even on the assumption that God exists.

MARY: What's that?

STEVE: Well, suppose that God suddenly decided to destroy all human minds. If parallelism were true, then what would change in the physical world?

DAVE: Absolutely nothing.

STEVE: Right, but surely this is a very bizarre consequence of any theory of mind.

MARY: Sure. If God destroyed all minds today, it would have no effect on the movements of human bodies tomorrow. We wouldn't have any thoughts, feelings, etc., but we would still go to our classes, write papers, and take our exams. All human physical behavior and interaction would continue in the same way despite the lack of any minds.

DAVE: Yeah, because if parallelism is true, minds have no causal bearing on or relevance to what happens in the physical world. All of our physical behavior would proceed unchanged despite the lack of any mentality behind it or caused by it.

MARY: So the ultimate point seems to be that, contrary to parallelism, we really do believe that there is mind-body causal interaction. Right?

DAVE: Yes, and that's why I opt for interactionism.

STEVE: Yes.

*　*　*　*　*　*　*　*　*　*　*　*

DAVE: Well, we've obviously reached the end of this discussion. I want to get clearer about your materialism, Mary. Your view is not without its own problems, you know.

STEVE: Yeah, good idea. Even though I sometimes lean toward materialism, I have a difficult time with certain aspects of it. That is why I hesitate to so openly declare myself a materialist. Let's put Mary on the spot.

MARY: Fine. What do you want to know?

DAVE: First of all, I'm not quite clear about your view. I understood what you said before, but you talk about "correlations" and "identities" in an often confusing way.

MARY: I hold that every mental state is a physical state or, more specifically, a neural state or brain process.

STEVE: But when you say 'is', do you mean 'is identical with'?

MARY: Of course. There aren't two different events, but merely two different names or descriptions for one brain event. Remember our discussion last night about co-referring terms?

STEVE: Yes, but can you give an example?

MARY: Sure. My current desire to drink some water is identical with some neural state in my brain. Of course I do not know exactly which neural state, but let's call whatever it is 'NS100'. It is the job of neuroscience to correlate mental states with brain states so that we can better discover the identities. We already have some idea about certain types of mental states, e.g. pain, emotions, memories, and visual experiences. Others will require more investigation, e.g. particular thoughts and complex higher-order cognitive capacities. But I am confident that we will eventually discover all of the relevant brain state correlations.

DAVE: This is your faith. I prefer mine.

MARY: Fine, but we have many analogous examples from the history of science. People knew about heat and water long before their scientific identity or explanation was discovered. The same goes for 'my desire to drink some water' and any mental state.

STEVE: But are you identifying events or properties?

MARY: How do you mean?

STEVE: Well, the *property* 'being water' is identified with the *property* 'being composed of H_2O'. This entails that anything that is water must be composed of H_2O. If something is not composed of H_2O, then it is not water. Is this what you mean to identify in the mind-brain case, i.e. the properties 'having a desire for water' and 'having NS100'?

MARY: Are you referring to what's called **'type-type' materialism**?

STEVE: Yes.

DAVE: Wait, what's that?

STEVE: As I said, it identifies mental types or properties with brain types or properties.

DAVE: So you are using 'type' and 'property' interchangeably?

STEVE: Yes, pretty much.

MARY: I'm not a type-materialist, although some philosophers of mind do hold this position.

DAVE: Why not?

MARY: Unlike the water and H_2O analogy, it seems possible for there to be conscious creatures who can have the desire to drink water but who do *not* have NS100. For example, if there are conscious beings on other planets, as seems very likely, they certainly wouldn't have the same kinds of brains that we do. They probably wouldn't have what we call 'neurons' at all. But I don't want to say that they couldn't have the desire to drink water unless they also have NS100. As a matter of fact, the brains of some animals on earth are perhaps different enough from ours so that even they will have different neural processes when they have such a desire. Mental states are multiply realized, i.e. the same mental type can be had by radically different creatures with very different physiologies. Type-materialism seems unwisely to rule this out.

DAVE: I see. Isn't this a very serious problem?

MARY: Many philosophers think so, and that's why many shy away from identifying mental types with specific physical types. If we identify the type 'having a desire to drink water' with the brain type 'NS100', then we seem committed to the idea that one must have NS100 in order to have that desire. But that seems much too strong.

STEVE: So you don't think that mental properties are identical with properties of human-like brains. Are you therefore a **'token-to-ken' materialist**?

MARY: I guess so.

DAVE: And what's token-materialism?

MARY: Well, it simply equates mental *events* with brain *events*. Events are particulars, e.g. a particular brain process or event inside someone's head.

DAVE: So now you are using 'token' and 'event' interchangeably?

MARY: Sure. Also, 'state' or 'process' is O.K. The idea is that any creature's mental state at time$_1$ is simply some physical or brain event *in that creature* at time$_1$. Every mental event is a physical event. You see how this avoids the multiple realizability problem facing the type-materialist.

DAVE: I think so, but tell me anyway.

MARY: My current desire to drink water is identical with NS100, which is some current physical event in me. But this does not rule out others having that type of mental state, even if they do not have NS100. Some alien creature can still have that same kind of desire, which, given its radically different physiology, would not be identical with NS100. But all the token-materialist claims is that the desire must be identical with one of *its* inner brain like events. And similarly for any mental state.

STEVE: I guess it's not quite that simple, however.

MARY: Well, no. There needs to be some connection to the typical input and the typical output or behavior associated with the mental state. Did you want to discuss that as well?

DAVE: Not really, unless Steve does.

STEVE: No, let's drop it here, because I really want to get into a serious puzzle involving materialism. I think I have a good idea of the view Mary is defending.

DAVE: I do too. What problem do you have in mind, Steve? Why don't you start? I may have one later.

*   *   *   *   *   *   *   *   *   *   *   *

STEVE: O.K. This is a problem about the inability of materialism to explain consciousness. We can call it 'the materialist problem of consciousness'. Here it goes. Let's suppose that we knew everything about the brain of a conscious lower animal, e.g. a cat or a bat. In other words, Mary, suppose that we did in fact have perfect knowledge about the brain.

MARY: Sounds great!

STEVE: We would therefore, according to materialism, have all of the third-person physical knowledge about the mind of a cat. Right?

MARY: Sure, because the cat's mind *is* its brain.

STEVE: O.K., but wouldn't a materialist say that we would have all of the facts about the cat's mind, period?

MARY: I suppose so, because we would know everything about its brain.

STEVE: But this is where the problem comes in. It seems obvious to me that there would still be something about the cat's mind that we did not know.

MARY: Like what?

STEVE: The way that cats experience the world, that is, what we might call 'what it is like to be a cat'. And the same would go for any other creature that is very different from us. We would not understand certain subjective facts about the cat's 'point of view' on the world, and we never could.

MARY: Maybe not, but why is this a problem for the materialist?

STEVE: Well, I understood materialism to say that *all* of the facts about someone's mind are physical facts. So if we knew everything about a brain, then we would know everything about a mind. But clearly this would not happen. Even if we had all of the scientific knowledge about a cat's brain, there would be many facts left out. These could only be 'mental facts' which are not reducible to the physical. That is, some things can only be known from the *subjective perspective*. Therefore, materialism is inherently flawed when it comes to explaining consciousness.

DAVE: I like that, Steve. And the crucial consequence for physical science, and for all those who treat it as a god, is that we could never come to know everything about the world through science. Even in an ideal future in which everything physical was known by us, something would still be left out of the story. Objective physical facts can be grasped from any point of view, but some facts are essentially limited to a subjective point of view. Steve's story reminds me of a similar argument.

MARY: Maybe, Dave, you should give your argument now. Then I can try to tackle both at once.

DAVE: O.K. Suppose, Mary, that your older sister Maria had been radically color-blind from birth so that she could only discern shades of white, grey, and black. Partly because of her condition and of hearing others talk about colors she can't see, she has become very interested in color perception.

MARY: Interesting; go on.

DAVE: Suppose further that, as in Steve's story, she learns everything about color perception in humans. Science has also advanced so much that she really knows everything about what goes on in normal humans when we perceive red. So Maria knows everything there is to know about the human brain and about color perception. That is, she has all of the neurophysiological information or knowledge about "having a red experience."

STEVE: I think I see where you are going.

MARY: Me too, so get there.

DAVE: Of course. Suppose further that a miraculous surgical technique becomes available that gives Maria normal color perception for the very first time. Now, immediately after the operation her eyes are covered with a bandage, which is subsequently removed by the doctor. It again just seems obvious that Maria comes to learn or know something new when she first looks at a red wall, namely, what it is like to have a red experience. And the same goes for any other color experience.

STEVE: Right. So we must ask: What did Maria learn upon seeing the red wall and upon having her first "reddish experience"? Since she already had all of the physical information, Maria must have gained some nonphysical information or some unique mental fact which could only be acquired by actually having the experience. So not all information or knowledge about the mind is physical information, and therefore materialism is false.

MARY: Very thought-provoking examples, but I don't think they spell doom for materialism. I'm sure there are many responses to them in the recent philosophical literature.

DAVE: O.K., but how would you respond now?

MARY: Three replies come to mind. Let me briefly explain them.

STEVE: Let's have number one.

MARY: *First*, in Maria's case, maybe she has been able to imagine what various colors would look like given her omniscience about the neuropsychology of color. She might have been able to "conjure up" reddish images in her mind because of what she knew. Just as we can picture or imagine objects without having experienced them, so Maria might have been able to do this with color experiences even before the surgery.

DAVE: Are you serious?

MARY: Sure. You must remember that, in your story, she knew *everything* about color perception. That's a lot! And we shouldn't underestimate what might follow from that fact. How can you be so sure that such a person wouldn't be able to imagine what certain colors would look like?

DAVE: I can't be absolutely sure, but it hardly seems likely. When we normally conjure up imaginary visual images, we only combine in our minds previously seen objects. But this is not so for Maria: she has never had any color experiences except for shades of black and white.

MARY: True, but I don't see how you could rule it out. It is very difficult to understand now just how much and what kind of knowledge we're talking about.

STEVE: Do you think something similar might be true about the cat story?

MARY: I'm not sure if it applies there. Of course if we knew everything about cat neurophysiology we would be better able to imagine what it is like to be a cat, but, because cat and human brains are so different and we just do not have cat brains, we probably would still fall short.

STEVE: Doesn't that concern you?

MARY: Not really. It brings me to my *second* reply: How did you get from the total knowledge about the cat's brain to a denial of materialism? You seem to be confusing epistemology, or a knowledge related claim, with the more metaphysical identity claim made by materialism.

STEVE: How do you mean?

MARY: Even if we were omniscient about cat neurophysiology but didn't know what it was like to be a cat, I don't see how this shows that the cat's mental states aren't just its brain states. Even Dave admitted last night that he believed materialism to be true for animals.

DAVE: Yes, but there remains the deeper problem of the explanatory limitations of materialism. Perhaps this is the primary lesson to be learned from Steve's cat story.

MARY: But materialism as a metaphysical claim about mind-brain identity seems unaffected. As a matter of fact, I think that our continuing puzzlement over cat experience should be expected. After all, only the cat is going through the experiences and is actually undergoing the brain processes.

Moreover, given that our brains are so different from cat brains, it seems natural for there to be certain aspects of their experience that we could never fully comprehend. I suspect this would be so for most cross-species cases. But I do not see how this refutes the central claim of materialism: mental states are neural or brain states.

DAVE: But how does this apply to my story about Maria?

MARY: Similarly, it would come as no surprise that she did not know 'what it is like to experience red' before the surgery. But that is because she was incapable, prior to the surgery, of undergoing the relevant brain processes despite all of her neurophysiological knowledge.

DAVE: So then you admit that Maria does learn something new after the surgery? And, if so, wouldn't it have to be something nonphysical?

MARY: No, and I'm not even sure that she does learn anything new. There are crucial ambiguities in your questions which make it seem as if materialism has a problem here.

DAVE: Like what? Does Maria learn something new or not?

MARY: This brings me to my *third* response, which is a bit more technical.

DAVE: We'll try to follow.

MARY: I'm sure you will. You talk about learning some new *fact* or *piece of information* in Maria's story. In short, you imply that she gains some further bit of knowledge when she experiences red for the first time.

DAVE: Yes.

MARY: But, first of all, we should distinguish between two types of knowledge: 'knowing that' or 'factual knowledge' which involves knowing that some fact or statement is true; and 'knowledge by acquaintance', which involves a more experiential type of knowing. For example, I know that Babe Ruth hit sixty home runs in a season, but I have no personal experience by which I acquired such knowledge. So, in this case, I know a *fact*, but I do not have knowledge by acquaintance of that same fact.

STEVE: O.K. I see the distinction, and I see how we could come up with many more examples. We often know that something is the case in the absence of direct knowledge by acquaintance.

MARY: Good. Well, Maria does *not* lack any factual knowledge about color perception. By your hypothesis she has it all! So she does not learn any new facts or information when she has her first experience of red.

DAVE: I'm not so sure about that. Doesn't she learn some new 'mental fact'?

MARY: I don't see why. If we found the tape of Babe Ruth's sixtieth home run during 1927 and watched it, would we come to learn some new fact about his home run total in 1927?

STEVE: I suppose not. We would only experience that same fact or event in a new way.

MARY: Exactly, and this also goes for Maria. After the surgery, Maria does not come to learn a new fact but only comes to know the same fact in a different way. She had the factual knowledge, and then comes to have knowledge by acquaintance of what it is like to have a reddish experience. But no new nonphysical mental fact is learned, and so there is no reason for the materialist to be embarrassed here. There isn't any 'mental' fact which eludes materialism, but only a different way to learn about that same fact through experience.

DAVE: Sounds strange to me. And I'm not sure about your Babe Ruth analogy. It just seems so obvious that Maria would have gained some additional knowledge not included in her prior physical knowledge.

MARY: But think of it in terms of last night's discussion. Remember Leibniz's Law, co-referring terms, first- and third-person perspectives, etc.?

DAVE: Sure.

MARY: From the third-person perspective, Maria is omniscient with respect to the relevant physical and neural properties. But then, after the surgery, she becomes acquainted with the same neural property from the first-person perspective, i.e. by undergoing the neural process herself. The neural property is not new; only the perspective is. Surely this is no threat to materialism.

STEVE: How do co-referring terms or expressions fit in?

MARY: There will always be at least two different names or expressions referring to the brain process responsible for a color experience. One will be in the language of neurophysiology, and the other in terms of a first-person description such as "the experience seems to me to be such-and-such." Before the surgery, Maria knew about the property only under the neurophysiological description. After the surgery, she comes to know about that same property under a first-person description. So why the big mystery?

STEVE: I'm not sure anymore. I need to think about it.

DAVE: Me too, but I still think there is something which materialism must always leave out in any explanation of conscious experience.

MARY: But even if materialism does have a real problem here, dualism is much worse off. Dave, you can't tell me that dualism can explain consciousness any better. Indeed, it would again seem impossible for dualism to explain it for some of the reasons we discussed last night. At least we are trying to explain consciousness.

STEVE: I agree with you on that, Mary.

DAVE: Maybe. But you, Mary, are the one who claims that you will be able to explain consciousness someday. So isn't it fair to ask where such a scientific investigation might lead and whether any problems would permanently persist?

MARY: Sure, but I think there are good replies to both of your examples.

STEVE: Perhaps. I have to go. Let's talk again tomorrow. I want to discuss something else.

DAVE: Same time, same place!

THE THIRD NIGHT

MARY: What do you want to discuss tonight?

DAVE: Steve had something in mind.

STEVE: Yes. Some of our conversation last night took on an epistemological tone, i.e. it dealt with issues of knowledge. I would like to discuss the so-called Problem of Other Minds, which is perhaps the most traditional epistemological problem in philosophy of mind.

DAVE: Good idea. Describe the basic problem as you see it.

STEVE: Actually, I think it's crucial to divide it into two subproblems or subquestions: (1) How can I know that another creature or thing has a conscious mind at all? and (2) How could I know whether another creature or thing has the same particular experiences or mental states that I do?

MARY: Yes. It's important to distinguish between these questions because I may be reasonably sure that you *have a mind* but more skeptical about whether or not you experience the world in the same way that I do. In other words, answering question (1) will often be easier than answering (2). We saw this last night when we talked about cats. We assumed that cats have conscious minds; the real problem has to do with what precisely their conscious experiences are like.

DAVE: Right, but in neither case will any such knowledge be as *certain* as the knowledge we have of our own minds. My knowledge that I have a conscious mind is about as certain as it gets. It is one of Descartes' indubitable truths. Of course, very few truths have such a lofty status, and very little knowledge is so absolutely certain.

MARY: Sure, and the problem is not limited to other *human* minds. We should also discuss various animal minds, aliens, and the idea that there could be conscious machines or robots. Our ability to answer questions (1) and (2) will no doubt depend greatly on which type of thing we are asking about. I have doubts about whether certain primitive creatures are conscious at all.

STEVE: I have doubts about the possibility of machine consciousness.

DAVE: Me too.

STEVE: But we often act as if we know about other minds. For example, I think I know that both of you have minds, especially after the last two nights. If I know this, how do I know it?

MARY: Well, Dave is right that this cannot be absolutely certain knowledge. But it can be some form of inductive knowledge based on good inductive reasoning. After all, most scientific knowledge is inductive and yet is not considered to be weakly grounded. For example, "all crows are black" and "the sun will rise tomorrow" are standard pieces of inductive knowledge based on past observation and strong evidence.

Good inductive reasoning will take evidence and show how it strongly supports the truth of a conclusion, even if it doesn't absolutely guarantee it. At the least, the evidence should show that the conclusion is *probably* or *very likely* to be true. The nature of the evidence will depend on what the inquiry is.

STEVE: Of course. If knowledge had to be "absolutely certain," then we would not know very much: perhaps only some truths about our own minds, mathematical truths, and some logical principles. In any case, we should at least strive for *rational belief* even if it falls short of knowledge, and we should always try to believe as rationally as possible. However, I do have serious doubts about how well we can answer the two subquestions.

MARY: I sometimes do too, but I also think that dualism has a more serious problem here.

DAVE: Why?

MARY: Well, according to dualism, another human mind could never be observed. But materialists believe that we do observe other minds, or at least it's possible to do so. So answering the problem is more difficult for you.

DAVE: Must you assume materialism here too?

MARY: I'm not assuming it. I'm just pointing out how much more difficult it is to acquire knowledge of other minds if dualism is true.

DAVE: But that's only if you assume that the brain is part of the evidence for the existence of another mind.

MARY: Of course! It seems to me that it would be very strong evidence for answering question (1). That is, if someone has a human or human-like brain, then it seems reasonable to believe that there is a conscious mind. Or at least it's very strong evidence for that conclusion. Don't you think so?

DAVE: I suppose so, but of course I do not believe that the mind just *is* the observed brain.

MARY: We know.

DAVE: But, anyway, don't you think you know now that I have a mind?

MARY: Sure.

DAVE: But if you do know it, your current knowledge cannot be based on any observation of my brain. You've never actually seen my brain.

MARY: No, but it seems reasonable to assume that it's in your skull because you appear from the outside to be a human being. It's no different from my clearly rational belief that you have lungs or a heart. And, again, it is at least possible for me to observe your mind or brain via X-ray, CAT-scan, or operation. But on your view we could never observe another human mind.

DAVE: Granted, but you must admit that as a matter of fact we do not often use brain observation as evidence for the existence of a mind.

*   *   *   *   *   *   *   *   *   *   *   *

STEVE: Enough of your own little debate. Many of my problems and questions apply equally to both of you. But first, in addition to brain structure, what other kinds of evidence can help us to deal with this problem?

MARY: Another would be behavioral reactions to stimuli or bodily movements. For example, the fact that you try to avoid bodily damage normally indicates that you expect to feel something. If I kick you in the leg, you will behave in a way that indicates the presence of consciousness. And, for that matter, the same goes for many animals, such as dogs and cats. This would be some evidence that another creature has a conscious mind and, in particular, the capacity to feel pain.

Last night we agreed that mental events cause bodily movements. So when we observe behavioral effects it is reasonable to infer the existence of some mental cause. I know this happens in my case, and it is reasonable to assume the same is true when I observe others behaving in similar ways.

DAVE: Right. Another piece of evidence has to do with the ability to use language or to communicate. It is partly on these grounds that I know you have a mind. We have communicated over the past two nights by using the English language. This seems to be good evidence that you have a conscious mind and in particular that you have conscious thoughts which you express through language. Even whales are able to communicate in their own way. Although they cannot communicate *with us*, they can with each other.

MARY: There are also three other related pieces of evidence which can help answer the problem of other minds.

STEVE: What are they?

MARY: They have to do with the ability to learn, the ability to solve problems, and creativity. For example, your ability to learn from our conversations or your ability to learn from a teacher provides some evidence that you have a conscious mind. Such an ability seems to require some kind of conscious memory and thought. Furthermore, you are able to solve problems in your everyday life. Even many lower animals when confronted with a challenging or unexpected situation are able to "figure out" what to do. Such an ability seems to require having a conscious thought process. As did early *Homo sapiens*, many lower animals have figured out ways to find food or to hunt, e.g. by making tools and weapons. And solving problems often involves a certain degree of creativity, which requires conscious thinking; for example, the human ability to build bridges or to write philosophical articles. Surely these show that one has a conscious mind.

DAVE: So let's agree that we have a solid list of four types of evidence which can help us to answer our original questions. Let's call them 'the four conditions' and number them as follows:

(1) Brain Structure
(2) Nonverbal or Nonvocal Behavioral Evidence
(3) Ability to Use Language and/or to Communicate
(4) Ability to Learn, Ability to Solve Problems, and/or Creativity

STEVE: O.K. You are both right that they are probably what we implicitly use when making judgments about whether or not another creature has a mind. But none of them individually can conclusively prove that another has a conscious mind.

MARY: How do you mean?

STEVE: Well, let's just look at the first subquestion: How can I know that another creature or thing has a conscious mind at all? Of course we must remember that our confidence in answering it will greatly depend on which "creature" or "thing" we're examining. So we really have many different questions. But if we take each of the four conditions individually, we will find that none of them can establish knowledge that another creature has a mind.

DAVE: Can you give counterexamples to each condition? In other words, can you think of cases where the evidence is present but where we would remain very skeptical about the existence of a conscious mind?

STEVE: Yes. Let's take each one. If another human has a brain structure similar to ours, how can we be sure that he is conscious? Suppose I show you a brain X-ray which resembles a typical human brain. You can't be sure that a conscious mind is associated with that brain.

MARY: Why not?

STEVE: It could be the brain of a coma patient or even of a recently deceased person. So there would be no consciousness.

DAVE: I'm sure that we can respond to that, but let's first hear about the other three conditions.

STEVE: O.K. The second condition also often falls short as being good evidence. Ants, flies, and insects display "avoidance behavior" when we try to kill them in our apartments, but I doubt that most of them are *consciously* thinking anything or are even capable of feeling pain.

Also, we may someday be able to build a robot that can behaviorally react in familiar ways. But I doubt if that would suffice to prove that robots have conscious minds. So appropriate behavioral reactions to stimuli cannot, by themselves, show that something has a conscious mind. Even a single-celled amoeba moves away from certain harmful fluids, but I don't know anyone who believes that a single cell could be conscious.

MARY: What about the last two conditions?

STEVE: Well, cognitive scientists and engineers often speak of computers as having a language and as communicating things to us. But I don't think that we should conclude that current computers are conscious. Also, you know that bees, for example, communicate to each other where honey can be found through a series of rather complicated "dances." Other bees are then informed as to the source of food.

MARY: Yes, it's a fascinating phenomenon.

STEVE: But it still seems rather doubtful that they are consciously relaying any such complicated thoughts.

MARY: Maybe, but go on.

STEVE: You talked about creativity. Perhaps it *often* indicates the presence of consciousness, but what about the way that spiders make their webs? It is an incredible phenomenon and one that seems to involve creativity in the way that they make different and very complex webs at different times. But I'm not sure that spiders are conscious creatures at all.

And the ability to learn or to solve problems is clearly not sufficient for consciousness. We can program computers to solve chess or mathematical problems, but no one believes that this is good evidence of a conscious mind. Actually, most computers can solve these problems better than humans. Also, rats and mice can "learn" many things through conditioning. But I'm not convinced that they are conscious, or at least that they are consciously remembering or thinking during the conditioning process.

DAVE: I don't agree with all of your claims, but even if we grant them for the sake of argument, you have only shown that none of the four conditions *individually* can *conclusively prove* that another creature has a conscious mind. And that is very weak.

STEVE: Why?

DAVE: Two reasons: First, we have already agreed that knowledge of other minds would at most be strongly inductive, i.e. it would only establish a likelihood that another has a conscious mind. "Absolute certainty" or "conclusive proof" is not the issue and is rarely achieved. *Strong evidence for a reasonable belief* is the issue. Remember?

STEVE: I suppose.

DAVE: Second, even if you are right that no single condition is, by itself, very strong evidence to support the conclusion that another has a mind, more than one condition would be, and, indeed, the more evidence or the more conditions met, the more likely that the creature in question has a conscious mind.

MARY: Yes! I like to think of it as a prosecutor trying to build a case against a defendant. There will rarely, if ever, be one single piece of evidence which conclusively proves his guilt. Perhaps a confession by the accused or convincing testimony by an eyewitness could, but the confession could have been coerced by a bad cop, or the eyewitness could simply have mistaken a similar looking person for the defendant.

STEVE: Sure. Even apparently damning evidence such as a fingerprint at the scene of the crime or possession of the murder weapon could involve an innocent person.

DAVE: Yeah, maybe the fingerprint was left on an earlier occasion and perhaps the murder weapon was planted by the real killer.

MARY: Anyway, my point is that many different pieces of evidence are required which when taken together strongly indicate the guilt of the defendant beyond a reasonable doubt, even if not beyond any doubt whatsoever. But in order to win the case the prosecutor will need to show, for example, evidence of motive, or opportunity, and some other evidence tying the defendant to the scene. In such cases, we justifiably say that we know the defendant is guilty. But no individual piece of evidence is sufficient to convict.

Similarly, in trying to determine whether another creature or object has a conscious mind, we must look at the whole range of evidence and the degree to which each type can be established. And this is what helps us to decide whether or not we have any such knowledge.

STEVE: O.K., but let's get down to specific examples.

MARY: Sure, let's start with human minds. How do I know that you or any other human has a conscious mind? You meet all four conditions. You presumably have a brain much like mine and this can be observed. Moreover, you display various behavioral reactions to stimuli, e.g. you avoid tripping over chairs. You also satisfy conditions three and four: you are able to use language to communicate and you demonstrate by your philosophical comments and arguments your creativity and your problem-solving ability. So I think I know that you and, by extension, any other human being has a conscious mind.

DAVE: And this would explain how your first counterexample can be answered.

STEVE: The one about the coma patient or the dead person?

DAVE: Yes. The reason we don't know that the coma patient or a dead person has a conscious mind has to do with conditions two, three, and four. These three conditions would not be satisfied. This should be obvious. Also, it isn't clear that even the first condition is satisfied, since we probably should take it to mean a properly *functioning* brain, not merely the brain structure itself.

STEVE: Of course, but small infants are not creative and cannot use language. Severely retarded humans also have difficulty meeting conditions three and four.

MARY: Yes, but they satisfy conditions one and two and really can communicate to some extent. So don't you think they meet enough conditions to warrant a claim of knowledge?

STEVE: I guess so, but you see that it gets complicated almost immediately.

MARY: Sure. I never said it would always be easy. But applying the four conditions is a useful strategy for dealing with the Problem of Other Minds.

DAVE: Let me also add a point here about their usefulness. At the other extreme, we might ask how we know that, say, rocks and plants are not conscious. The answer is that they do not meet any of the four conditions. That is, a rock does not have a brain or anything like a nervous system. Nor does it behaviorally react in the way that conscious creatures do when kicked or stepped on. Neither do rocks try to avoid potentially "painful" experiences. The same goes for plants and trees: they don't jump out of the way when we cut them or scream when a saw gets near them. There is also no reason to believe that rocks or plants use language or communicate to us or to one another. Finally, the fourth condition is clearly not satisfied: rocks or plants do not learn anything and display no ability to solve problems.

STEVE: Sure. I am not saying that the four conditions are useless. But the real hard questions have to do with the "in-between" cases. Perhaps we clearly know that other humans are conscious and that plants and rocks are not, but what about the unclear cases where only some or most of the conditions are met? And what about when the evidence conflicts?

MARY: Such as?

STEVE: Let's go back to my earlier examples. The behavior of certain flies and insects may suggest consciousness, but I seriously doubt that most of them are conscious creatures.

MARY: Well, this is a case where the creature probably does not satisfy the other three conditions. Flies and worms, for example, do not have anything like a true brain with extensive neurons and a nervous system. They also clearly fail to meet conditions three and four. So we might agree that flies are not conscious because they fail to meet most of the conditions. At least we would have an explanation. Some primitive creatures may have evolved in a purely nonconscious way. Moths would be another good example. If we go by the evidence, we should seriously doubt that they are conscious.

DAVE: And your single-celled organism can be explained in a similar way. It should be obvious that amoebas cannot satisfy conditions one, three, and four.

STEVE: Fine, but are you saying you know that such things are not conscious?

DAVE: In some cases, yes. For example, the evidence is overwhelming against rocks and plants, so it is reasonable to claim that we know they lack consciousness. I think we can say the same about single-celled organisms and most insects. At the least, we can justifiably assert that it is highly unlikely. That is, it is reasonable to believe that they do not have conscious minds.

STEVE: How about my bee example?

MARY: That's a bit tougher because bees seem to satisfy two of the four conditions. Like flies and insects, they meet condition two, and in addition they seem to have the rather sophisticated ability to communicate that you mentioned earlier. So condition three seems satisfied to some extent, but conditions one and four remain in serious doubt.

STEVE: I agree, so what's your solution here?

MARY: I confess I'm not sure about whether we can know that a bee has a conscious mind. That is, whether we could know either way. But one possibility is that, when the evidence is divided, we should ask whether one condition should carry more weight than the others. This way we can better form a reasonable opinion. I am inclined to use brain structure as the "tie breaker." Bees do not really have much of a brain or nervous system, and so it is difficult to see how consciousness is possible.

DAVE: Much the same goes for spiders. They clearly meet condition two, but I doubt if they meet conditions one and three. Steve had claimed that they satisfy condition four because they display some creative ability in making webs.

Mary: Right, spiders are in that grey area with bees. The difference is that the former display a creativity lacking in the latter, whereas bees communicate in rather sophisticated ways.

Dave: Yes, but I sometimes wonder if a spider's ability to make webs really deserves to be called "creative." Such behavior may just be purely nonconscious innate activity that does not require any conscious thinking or planning at all. So perhaps we should conclude that spiders are not conscious since they really only satisfy the second condition.

Steve: How would the four conditions apply to other animals?

Dave: Well, apes and gorillas would clearly satisfy all four conditions. Their brains are similar enough to ours, although they do not have as much cerebral cortex, the brain area responsible for our more sophisticated mental abilities. They often react as we do to external stimuli. They also at least have some ability to communicate with us and especially with one another, to use primitive languages, and to solve certain limited problems.

Mary: Right, and we're not saying that they satisfy conditions three and four to the same degree as humans. But the overall evidence seems sufficient to establish that they are conscious creatures.

Steve: I suppose so. I guess the same would go for animals such as lions, bears, tigers, cats, and dogs.

Mary: I think so, even though the evidence will perhaps be somewhat weaker. For example, a cat brain is not nearly as sophisticated as an ape brain. Also, cats surely do not have the same communication or learning abilities as higher mammals. But I don't think that this should cause us to doubt that they have conscious minds.

Dave: And dogs, for example, can be trained to do some rather amazing things which go well beyond mere "conditioning." Just think about the mental abilities required for being a seeing-eye or police dog.

Steve: Fair enough, but aside from insects, are there any other animals or creatures which you really doubt are conscious at all? That is, which animals do you think are not likely to be conscious?

DAVE: Sometimes I wonder about mice and frogs for some of the reasons mentioned concerning bees and spiders. But I would bet that they are capable of having at least some primitive conscious mental states.

MARY: I am very skeptical about turtles, snakes, and many types of fish. However, I know that even they have more advanced brains than is sometimes believed. So I tend to give them the benefit of the doubt, although I am not as confident about some very small types of fish.

STEVE: So then you do admit that it is difficult to answer the first subquestion regarding many lower animals or creatures.

MARY: Sure. I don't want to give the impression that I have all the answers, even using the four conditions as our basis. But I do think that it is still the best strategy for dealing with the Problem of Other Minds.

STEVE: But of course you must admit that the problem only gets more difficult when we try to answer the second subquestion: How could I know that another creature or thing has the same particular experiences or mental states that I do? Even if we can know that a cat has a conscious mind, we saw last night that it is much more difficult to know precisely what a cat's conscious experience is like at a particular time. And the same would go for many of the other animals we have discussed tonight.

DAVE: I agree with that. After all, even if we know that a certain animal is conscious, we would not know what it is consciously experiencing at any given time.

STEVE: Right. How do we know what a dog feels when we step on its paw? How do we know what a lion is thinking or feeling while it is chasing a deer? How do we know what it is like for an eagle to soar over the cliffs? How could I know what kind of visual experience my dog is having as it sits next to me on my porch? And so on and so on. We surely cannot assume that they experience things in the same way that we do.

MARY: Maybe not, but perhaps we can look to the four conditions for *some* help. For example, a dog's reaction when we step on its paw seems to indicate that it feels something very unpleasant, probably much as we do when someone steps on our bare foot. This would provide further evidence since dogs also share with us some lower brain structure.

STEVE: But conditions three and four are useless here. For example, no animal can ever really tell us what its experience is like. We simply interpret its behavior as best we can.

DAVE: And even the first condition might often be unhelpful. It can help *rule out* the possibility that a creature has a certain type of conscious state because it simply lacks the relevant brain structure. But merely knowing that an animal has a visual cortex of a certain kind cannot tell us very much about its specific moment-to-moment visual experiences.

MARY: I agree that this is a more difficult problem, but I am a bit more optimistic, especially to the extent that the neurosciences can help.

*   *   *   *   *   *   *   *   *   *   *   *

STEVE: Well, anyway, I want to discuss the problem in another way. Let's talk about aliens. Suppose a UFO landed on earth and three little things emerged. How would we know whether they are purely nonconscious sophisticated robots sent by intelligent life on another planet or whether they are conscious creatures? I don't think that the answer would be easy.

MARY: Why not? Let's say that we were able to capture them and observe them for a long period of time in a large scientific lab. No doubt everyone would be interested in observing them: philosophers, psychologists, neuroscientists. I think it would make the front page! Why wouldn't we be able to gather enough information to make a reasonable judgment?

STEVE: Well, maybe we could in some cases, but look at the four conditions we have been using. Looking inside their "heads" at "brain structure" would probably be useless.

MARY: Why? It might show that there really is no "brain" at all, but rather something more mechanical or machine-like.

STEVE: Maybe, but how could we tell whether that "something" could sustain consciousness?

MARY: Well, this is a difficult separate question which we can discuss later. But let's assume for now that the creature has something complex enough to be called a brain as we typically use the word. It seems that we would then be fairly sure that the alien is conscious.

STEVE: But what basis could we have for judging that the "brain structure" of the alien does or does not provide evidence of consciousness? We all agreed last night that alien brains would probably be radically different from ours. After all, aliens would be from a very different environment and probably composed of radically different kinds of matter. This was part of your reason for not embracing type-materialism. Remember?

MARY: Yes, but it still seems possible to determine if a creature even with a very different brain is conscious.

STEVE: I don't see how. We would have nothing to compare it to in order make such a judgment. We can't tell just by watching a complicated thing function. It's not as if the conscious states are revealed through our observation. Even in our own case, we only know that other humans and animals are conscious because we have a similar brain. But in the alien case no such comparison can be made. How could we know whether the creature was not merely some very intelligent complex machine?

DAVE: Good question. I have to agree with Steve's skepticism here. I don't think it would be so easy to tell, even after extensive observation. And materialism won't help here.

STEVE: Right, because you can't just observe or see that the alien has a conscious mind even if you believe that all mental processes are physical processes. We are trying to figure out whether the alien has a conscious mind in the first place.

MARY: Maybe we wouldn't know just by looking at the inside of its "head," but what about the other evidence?

STEVE: I think we run into similar problems with the other three conditions. It wouldn't be like *Star Trek*, where all of the aliens look and behave very much like us, and where many of them even speak English! Amazing! Conditions two and three would almost be useless. We would likely have no way of communicating with them. Nor could we easily interpret their bodily reactions. How could we possibly know what is their "typical" or "normal" reaction to certain stimuli? And even if we could know, why would we expect it to be anything like ours?

MARY: Good questions, but over time we might be able to determine the way they normally react to certain stimuli and go from there. For example, they may not do what we normally do in the presence of intense heat, but we can observe what they do over a long period of time.

STEVE: And then what? If they do nothing, we cannot conclude that it is because they are not conscious, because heat might not affect them in the way it affects us. Maybe they come from a much hotter planet. And if they do react in a rather predictable way, it may only be a built-in nonconscious reaction, like that of a sophisticated robot that has been programmed to avoid a dangerous heat source.

MARY: Maybe, but then we should go on to see how they react to very cold temperatures. Perhaps this would cause them to react differently if they are from a hot planet. I mean, the evidence would take time to build up and analyze, but I think we could eventually form a rather reasonable conclusion. Some evidence might help to rule out consciousness and other evidence would support it. Also, you ignored condition four. Wouldn't we be able to determine whether the alien had learning or creative abilities through various testing techniques?

STEVE: Perhaps, but this wouldn't show that it is *consciously* learning or doing anything. Maybe it is a purely nonconscious robot with excellent learning abilities and built-in intelligence. We haven't been able to make such a robot yet, but extraterrestrial beings may have been.

DAVE: Sounds right to me. And even if we became confident enough to answer subquestion one in a positive way, do you both see how much more difficult it is to answer the second subquestion?

STEVE: Of course; that would be almost impossible. I mean, even if we were fairly sure that the alien had a conscious mind, it would be much more difficult to know how it experiences the world at any given moment. For example, what colors does it see?

MARY: Sure, that would be a problem, especially since their brains would not be similar to ours in any way.

DAVE: Right.

*　*　*　*　*　*　*　*　*　*　*　*

MARY: But it occurs to me that you have both assumed that no "machine" or "robot" could be conscious. I'm not so sure that we should rule out this possibility even if we cannot build one now. Why do you?

STEVE: One reason is that they do not have organic brains at all. That is, they are not composed of the kind of matter necessary for conscious experience. I don't see how things made out of computer chips, metal, and wires could be conscious.

MARY: But you and Dave have also said that you can't understand how electro-chemical reactions inside our skulls could achieve the same result. Maybe consciousness can be realized in all kinds of radically different substances.

STEVE: I don't see how substances like metal and computer chips could underlie consciousness or genuine "thinking." There just seems to be something very different about them.

MARY: You can't be sure about that. Why can't that type of physical substance give rise to consciousness? You really haven't said.

DAVE: Maybe it has to do with the idea that only organisms can be conscious. That is, organisms as opposed to artifacts.

STEVE: How do you distinguish them?

DAVE: Well, organisms are individuals in an enduring species; they take in food and excrete wastes; they are non-rigid physical objects; they reproduce through sexual intercourse; etc. Artifacts, on the other hand, are built by organisms. Being an organism is necessary for consciousness. And since robots and machines are not organisms, they cannot be conscious.

MARY: Interesting how you suddenly rely on all these biological facts. Perhaps we are reluctant to attribute consciousness to machines for this reason. But this would rule out God as conscious if you take it literally. See why?

DAVE: Well, yes, but I don't want to get into that. Why can't you allow for a unique exception and still appreciate my distinction?

MARY: I appreciate your point, but you fail to appreciate its consequences for theism. Anyway, I agree with you that this may be a factor in judging whether something has a conscious mind. Moreover, it sheds some light on our previous discussion concerning aliens.

STEVE: How so?

MARY: You have repeatedly pointed out that the issue came down to whether the beings which emerged from the UFO were actually alien creatures or merely sophisticated robots. Perhaps that's the key question: Are the creatures organisms or robots? If they are organisms, then they are likely to be conscious. If not, then perhaps they are less likely to be conscious. I say "perhaps" because I am not as skeptical as you are about the possibility of machine consciousness.

But aside from lacking an organic brain, why else should we rule out machine consciousness?

DAVE: I have a second reason. Machines do not really understand anything that is going on inside them. There is merely the manipulation of symbols and programmed functioning, but no real understanding of internal processes. In short, a machine does not understand the meaning of anything it processes.

STEVE: You mean in the way we consciously understand the workings of our own minds through introspection?

DAVE: Sure. Suppose we could make a robot that serves as an excellent translator of German. Whenever it is given an English sentence as input it responds with the perfect German translation as output. It can also answer questions flawlessly regarding German and English. Would we say that the robot *understands* or *knows* German? Of course not.

STEVE: I agree. This is related to conditions two and three. If we built a robot which non-verbally and verbally behaved as we do in giving correct German translations, we should still not say that it understands German. This clear lack of understanding on the part of the robot itself is good reason to doubt that it is conscious.

MARY: Well, I'm not sure that we shouldn't properly attribute some form of "understanding" to the robot.

DAVE: Really? Does a chess machine really understand the rules of chess? Does a calculator understand mathematics?

MARY: Maybe not, but if there were a robot that was behaviorally indistinguishable from humans in all or most respects, then it would be reasonable. I'm not saying there is such a robot now, but surely there could be.

DAVE: I don't see how, especially if you mean anything like a conscious "understanding."

STEVE: I agree with Dave, especially given our other earlier reason. If we knew that the robot was made of computer chips and metal, then that alone should cause us to doubt its capacity for conscious thought and understanding.

MARY: Well, what more can I say?

* * * * * * * * * * * *

STEVE: We did seem to agree earlier that the second subquestion is very difficult, if not impossible, to answer regarding aliens and even some lower animals.

DAVE: Sure.

MARY: Especially for aliens.

STEVE: But I think that this problem is almost as serious with respect to other humans. Even if we are confident that other humans have conscious minds, there remains one special kind of skepticism.

MARY: What?

STEVE: Well, one way of putting the problem is this: How do I know, for example, that you have the same color experience that I do when I am perceiving a ripe tomato? I know what my inner color experience is like, but can I know that yours is anything like mine?

DAVE: Surely it's reasonable to assume that we all have the same kind of "reddish" color experience.

STEVE: I don't think so.

MARY: Why not?

STEVE: Let me put it this way. Pretend that we have a ripe tomato and a lemon on this table. When I perceive the tomato I know what my color experience is like and I call it 'red'; and when I look at the lemon I know what that experience is like and I call it 'yellow'. But how do I or could I know that when you perceive these items you are having the same kinds of inner experiences? In fact, how do I know that your color experiences are not the opposite of mine or "inverted" with respect to mine?

MARY: You mean that I might perceive the lemon color the way that you perceive the tomato color?

STEVE: Yes, and vice versa. And perhaps there are many humans who perceive colors in this inverted way. How could we know otherwise?

DAVE: Interesting. I see what you mean. I assume this problem could arise in terms of the other senses.

STEVE: Sure. I could have talked about "taste inversion" by using different flavors, or discussed "hearing inversion" by using different sounds. But let's stick to visual color inversion. This is called the 'inverted spectrum problem'.

MARY: But don't we know the answer on the basis of verbal behavior?

STEVE: Such as?

MARY: We all say that the tomato looks red like blood; not yellow like the sun. If you ask me what color the tomato is, I will say 'red', just as you will.

STEVE: But that's only what we say. I am talking about the inner color *experience*, not the *name* we use for it. All I would know is that you use the word 'red' to describe what you perceive the color of a tomato to be, but I know nothing about what your color experience itself is like.

DAVE: That's true. After all, how are we taught color terms?

STEVE: Exactly. We put different objects in front of children and teach them to associate color terms with them. For example, a child is told that a tomato or a fire truck is red, and a lemon and the sun are yellow. And so on. But this tells us nothing about how these objects appear to the children in their own subjective experience. So we all grow up using the words in a consistent way, but we have no basis for knowing that our color experiences are the same.

DAVE: So what Mary might call 'red' when she looks at the tomato could still appear to her the way that lemons appear to us.

STEVE: Sure. You see how difficult it is to know otherwise?

MARY: But wouldn't there be other evidence that could help decide the issue?

STEVE: Like what? After all, it is difficult to explain to another person what a color looks like. Try it sometime.

MARY: True, but we might associate other words and even some emotions with the experience of a certain color.

DAVE: For example?

MARY: We might say that some colors are light, dark, strong, weak, dull, bright, etc. So if we hear two people comparing color experiences, we should be able to make substantial headway.

DAVE: You mean like ruling out a 'brown-red' inversion by asking them which object looks 'bright' or 'dark'?

MARY: Yeah, something like that. If they agree on which object looks bright, then we certainly have good evidence for their having similar color experiences. Right?

STEVE: Maybe, but it wouldn't work for our 'yellow-red' case. And the point made earlier goes for how we learn these words. We are taught to associate the term 'bright' with red and yellow experiences and 'dark' with brown color experiences. But, once again, we have no clue as to what another's experience itself is like.

MARY: But don't you think this problem could be overcome? I mean, are there whole groups of painters and artists out there experiencing the world in such radically different ways? I find that hard to believe. Wouldn't there have to be some outward sign of it?

STEVE: I'm not so sure. But, anyway, we obviously don't normally quiz each other in order to find out such things. So our knowledge of another human's color experience is rather shaky. I can't think of any other way to help us deal with the problem.

MARY: Perhaps neurophysiological evidence can help settle the issue.

DAVE: How?

MARY: We have good evidence that certain neurons and "cones" are typically involved in the visual processing of certain types of color experience.

DAVE: So?

MARY: Well, if another human being's brain works the way ours does while looking at the ripe tomato, it seems reasonable to conclude that he is having a similar kind of "reddish" experience. I mean, if neurons fire in those same areas all across the human species, doesn't that point to a similarity in the experiences themselves?

DAVE: I don't see why. First of all, when we look at another's brain, we don't actually see the color as he perceives it. All we see is the brain which is the same color through and through; it's not as if those neurons become red when they fire.

MARY: Of course, but there is the association between the neural firings and that type of color experience.

DAVE: But we must eventually rely on the subject's verbal reports in order to make the correlations. And so we end up right back with the same old problem.

MARY: Really? I would think that such a uniform objective fact about human brains would outweigh any doubt arising from our earlier problem.

STEVE: Maybe it would, but I don't know how strongly to weigh such evidence. Also, we might then ask: How do we know that all human brains are "wired" in the same way? Maybe a good percentage of humans have brains in which the neurons that typically underlie red experiences instead underlie yellow experiences. That is, maybe some human brains themselves are wired in an inverted way. We certainly can't know otherwise by simply looking at them. As Dave said, we won't see the color of the person's experience simply by observing the relevant neural firings.

MARY: This sounds crazy to me, but I see your concern. Anyway, I'm a bit tired. I think I'll go home. Maybe I'll stare at my nice *red* carpet for a while and think about this some more.

DAVE: O.K. I'll give you both a ride home if you want. I haven't been drinking.

STEVE: Good. Thanks. Let's talk again some other time. I'm looking forward to taking more graduate courses in philosophy of mind.

MARY: Me too.

STUDY QUESTIONS

The First Night

1. What is materialism? What is substance dualism? Why does Mary believe that it is almost impossible for a materialist to believe in immortality? Why is a dualist in a better position to believe in immortality?

2. Do you agree with Mary that it is difficult to make any coherent distinction between the mind and the soul? Why or why not?

3. Explain in some detail the three general scientific reasons Mary gives in favor of materialism. Do you find these reasons compelling? Which do you think is the strongest? Does Dave satisfactorily respond? Why or why not?

4. State and explain the Divisibility Argument for dualism. Explain the role of Leibniz's Law in the argument. Discuss in some detail several objections to it, paying special attention to the 'imagine/conceive' and the 'first-person/third-person' distinctions. Does Dave satisfactorily respond? Why or why not?

5. State and explain the Argument from Introspection. Explain the role of Leibniz's Law in the argument. Discuss in some detail the two major objections to it, paying special attention to the failure of Leibniz's Law in intensional contexts. Can Dave satisfactorily respond? Why or why not?

The Second Night

1. What is interactionism? Explain, in general, why Mary believes that materialism can explain mind-body interaction far better than dualism can.

2. Explain in some detail the two more specific and major objections to interactionism, paying special attention to the relevance of the Conservation of Energy Principle. Does Dave satisfactorily respond to either objection? Why or why not?

3. What scientific experiments could help settle the materialism-dualism dispute?

4. Why does Steve think that evidence from brain damage might refute dualism? Does Dave satisfactorily respond? Why or why not?

5. What is parallelism? Why doesn't Dave consider it the right version of dualism? Explain several other objections to parallelism.

6. What is type-materialism? Why doesn't Mary believe that this is the correct version of materialism? What is token-materialism? How does it avoid the major problem with type-materialism?

7. In general terms, what is the materialist problem of consciousness? Explain in some detail the two stories used by Dave and Steve to illustrate this problem. How does Mary respond to each story? Specifically, what three responses does she offer? Does she successfully respond? Why or why not? Can you think of any other possible responses?

The Third Night

1. What is the problem of other minds? What are the two sub-problems and why is it important to distinguish between them?

2. What is inductive knowledge? Why is it relevant to the Problem of Other Minds?

3. Why does Mary think that the problem of other minds is more difficult to solve for a dualist? Is she right? Why or why not?

4. Describe the four conditions or types of evidence presented that can help us to solve the problem of other minds. Which do you think is strongest? Why? Which do you think is weakest? Why?

5. How does Steve try to attack each of the four conditions? How do Mary and Dave eventually reply to Steve's examples? What is the relevance of Mary's analogy of the prosecutor building a case against a defendant?

6. Can we know that other humans have conscious minds? On what grounds?

7. Can we know that animals have conscious minds? If so, which animals and on what grounds? Which animals or insects are you most skeptical about? Why?

8. Explain Steve's story about the aliens. Would we be able to determine whether or not they are conscious creatures? Why or why not?

9. Why do Steve and Dave doubt that a machine or robot can be conscious? Does Mary satisfactorily respond? Why or why not? Who do you think is closer to the truth?

10. Explain the inverted spectrum problem. Why is it most relevant to the second subproblem? Does Mary satisfactorily respond? Why or why not? Can you think of any other responses?

NOTES AND SUGGESTIONS FOR FURTHER READING

Introductory Books:

Jerome Shaffer (1968), *Philosophy of Mind* (Prentice Hall, Inc.).

Colin McGinn (1982), *The Character of Mind* (Oxford University Press).

Keith Campbell (1984), *Body and Mind* (University of Notre Dame Press).

Paul M. Churchland (1988), *Matter and Consciousness* (MIT: Bradford Books).

William Bechtel (1988), *Philosophy of Mind* (Lawrence Erlbaum).

Stephen Priest (1991), *Theories of the Mind* (Houghton Mifflin Co.).

Barbara Hannan (1994), *Subjectivity and Reduction* (Westview Press).

Advanced Anthologies:

Ned Block ed. (1980), *Readings in Philosophy of Psychology*, Vol. 1 (Harvard University Press).

William Lycan ed. (1990), *Mind and Cognition* (Basil Blackwell).

David Rosenthal ed. (1991), *The Nature of Mind* (Oxford University Press).

Advanced Books:

David M. Armstrong (1968), *A Materialist Theory of the Mind* (Routledge and Kegan Paul).

Owen Flanagan (1984), *The Science of the Mind* (MIT: Bradford Books).

Patricia S. Churchland (1986), *Neurophilosophy* (MIT: Bradford Books).

Christopher Hill (1991), *Sensations: A Defense of Type Materialism* (Cambridge University Press).

Daniel Dennett (1991), *Consciousness Explained* (Little, Brown and Co.).

John Searle (1992), *The Rediscovery of the Mind* (MIT: Bradford Books).

Owen Flanagan (1992), *Consciousness Reconsidered* (MIT: Bradford Books).

John Heil (1992), *The Nature of True Minds* (Cambridge University Press).

Books on the Related Problem of *Personal Identity* Include:

John Perry ed. (1975), *Personal Identity* (University of California Press).

Amelie Rorty ed. (1976), *The Identities of Persons* (University of California Press).

John Perry (1978), *A Dialogue on Personal Identity and Immortality* (Hackett Publishing Company).

James Baillie (1993), *Problems in Personal Identity* (Paragon House).

Notes:

(1) Concerning most of the issues raised in this dialogue, any of the introductory books or advanced anthologies would be an excellent place to begin for further reading.

For more on Descartes' early dualist arguments, see his *Meditations on First Philosophy*, translated by Donald A. Cress (Hackett Publishing Company, 1979). For a more recent defense of interactionism, see Karl R. Popper and John C. Eccles (1977), *The Self and Its Brain* (Routledge and Kegan Paul).

(2) For more on the "Argument from Introspection" and Leibniz's Law as discussed in the First Night, see Paul Churchland 1988, chapter two.

(3) Dave's story about Maria in the Second Night was intentionally modeled after Frank Jackson's story about Mary in "Epiphenomenal Qualia" (1982), *The Philosophical Quarterly*, 13, pp. 23–40, which is reprinted in Lycan 1990. See also F. Jackson's "What Mary Didn't Know," reprinted in Rosenthal 1991.

(4) Steve's story about the cat in the Second Night was modeled after Thomas Nagel's argument in "What Is It Like to Be a Bat?" (1974), *Philosophical Review*, 83, pp. 435–50, which is reprinted in Block 1980 and Rosenthal 1991. See also T. Nagel (1986), *The View from Nowhere* (Oxford University Press).

(5) For a sample of some rather sophisticated materialist replies to Jackson, Nagel, and to what I have called 'the materialist problem of consciousness', see:

T. Horgan (1984), "Jackson on Physical Information and Qualia," *Philosophical Quarterly*, 34, pp. 147–52.

Paul Churchland (1985), "Reduction, Qualia and the Direct Introspection of Brain States," *Journal of Philosophy*, 82, pp. 2–28.

R. Van Gulick (1985), "Physicalism and the Subjectivity of the Mental," *Philosophical Topics*, 16, pp. 51–70.

M. Tye (1986), "The Subjective Qualities of Experience," *Mind*, 95, pp. 1–17.

D. Lewis (1990), "What Experience Teaches," reprinted in Lycan 1990.

(6) For more on the traditional "problem of other minds," see the selections under the heading "Knowing Other Minds" in Rosenthal 1991.

(7) For more on animal mentality and consciousness, see:

Jonathan Bennett (1988), "Thoughtful Brutes," *Proceedings and Addresses of the American Philosophical Association*, 62, pp. 197–210.

Jonathan Bennett (1989), *Rationality* (Hackett Publishing Company). Originally published in 1964.

Dorothy Cheney and Robert Seyfarth (1990), *How Monkeys See the World* (University of Chicago Press).

Donald Griffin (1992), *Animal Minds* (University of Chicago Press).

Rocco J. Gennaro (1993), "Brute Experience and the Higher-Order Thought Theory of Consciousness," *Philosophical Papers*, 22, pp. 51–69.

(8) For more on the problem of machine consciousness and artificial intelligence, see:

John Searle (1980), "Minds, Brains and Programs," *The Behavioral and Brain Sciences*, 3, pp. 417–24.

John Searle (1984), *Minds, Brains and Science* (Harvard University Press).

John Haugeland (1985), *Artificial Intelligence: The Very Idea* (MIT: Bradford Books).

Margaret Boden ed. (1990), *The Philosophy of Artificial Intelligence* (Oxford University Press).

Jay Garfield ed. (1990), *Foundations of Cognitive Science* (Paragon House).

(9) Dave's story about the robot German translator in the Third Night is based on John Searle's (1980) well-known Chinese room argument.

(10) For more on the inverted spectrum problem, see:

J. Levine (1983), "Materialism and Qualia: The Explanatory Gap,"
    Pacific Philosophical Quarterly, 64, pp. 354–61.

T. Horgan (1984), "Functionalism, Qualia and the Inverted Spectrum,"
    Philosophy and Phenomenological Research, 44, pp. 453–69.

M. Tye (1986), "The Subjective Qualities of Experience," *Mind*, 95, pp. 1–
    17.

C. L. Hardin (1987), "Qualia and Materialism: Closing the Explanatory
    Gap," *Philosophy and Phenomenological Research*, 48, pp. 281–98.

INDEX OF KEY TERMS